The New York Times

Guide to
Marketing

Jamie Murphy

Edward J. Forrest
Head, School of Marketing
Griffith University–Queensland, Australia

IVCCD Libraries
MCC B. J. Harrison Library
Marshalltown, Iowa 50158

Australia • Canada • Denmark • Japan • Mexico • New Zealand • Philippines
Puerto Rico • Singapore • South Africa • Spain • United Kingdom • United States

The New York Times Guide to Marketing, by Jamie Murphy & Edward J. Forrest

Publisher: Dave Shaut
Acquisitions Editor: Pamela M. Person
Marketing Manager: Rob Bloom
Production Editor: Elizabeth A. Shipp
Media and Technology Editor: Kevin von Gillern
Media Production Editor: Robin K. Browning
Manufacturing Coordinator: Sandee Milewski
Internal Design: Joe Devine
Cover Design: Joe Devine
Copyeditor: Brian L. Massey
Production House: Trejo Production
Printer: Webcom

Copyright © 2001, South-Western College Publishing, a division of Thomson Learning. The Thomson Learning logo is a registered trademark used herein under license.

Copyright © 2001, The New York Times Company. Used by permission of The New York Times Company. All rights reserved.

All Rights Reserved. No part of this work covered by the copyright hereon may be reproduced or used in any form or by any means—graphic, electronic, or mechanical, including photocopying, recording, taping, or information storage and retrieval systems—without the written permission of the publisher.
   Printed in Canada
   1 2 3 4 5 02 01 00 99

For more information contact South-Western College Publishing, 5101 Madison Road, Cincinnati, Ohio, 45227 or find us on the Internet at http://www.swcollege.com
For permission to use material from this text or product, contact us by
• **telephone: 1-800-730-2214**
• **fax: 1-800-730-2215**
• **web: http://www.thomsonrights.com**

Library of Congress Cataloging-in-Publication Data

Murphy, Jamie, 1950–
   The New York Times guide to marketing / Jamie Murphy, Edward J. Forrest.
      p. cm.
   ISBN 0-324-04182-9 (alk. paper)
   1. Marketing.   I. Forrest, Edward J. II. Title.

HF5415.M8345 2001
658.8--dc21   99-049442

This book is printed on acid-free paper.

PREFACE

The New York Times Guide to Marketing is designed for students, professors and business professionals—anyone interested in staying current in business today. A collection of the best marketing-related articles from the *New York Times*, this guide does more than inform: it also provides context for the effects of change on all aspects of business. Also included are articles from *CyberTimes*, the online-only technology section of the *New York Times on the Web*. Each article was selected for its relevance to today's business world.

In purchasing **The New York Times Guide to Marketing**, you are not only purchasing the contents between the covers, but also unlimited access, via password, to related *New York Times* articles. Current articles will be linked from the South-Western College Publishing/*New York Times* Web site (http://nytimes.swcollege.com) on an ongoing basis as news breaks.

This guide can be used formally in the classroom or informally for life-long learning. All articles are accompanied by exploratory exercises and probing questions developed by experts in the field. Previews provide context for each chapter of articles and link them to key marketing principles. This guide is divided into eight sections organized to highlight the eight most critical factors in marketing today. This organization allows for easy integration into any marketing course.

Chapter 1: The Field of Marketing. This opening chapter introduces the nature, role and scope of the marketing discipline and its main concept and processes. Topics include: definitions, evolution, importance, role and scope, the marketing concept and ethical considerations.

Chapter 2: Marketing Management. A lesson in strategic planning and crisis management helps you understand the role of marketing in today's society. Topics include: marketing management process, strategic marketing planning, strategic alliances, radical marketing, the marketing plan, planning and implementing, evaluating marketing performance and crisis management

Chapter 3: The Marketing Environment. As this chapter demonstrates, successful marketers must constantly scan the internal and external elements that could impact their business. Topics include: environmental monitoring, external macro-environment, economic conditions, competition, external micro-environment, internal micro-environment, evaluating marketing opportunities and legal environment.

Chapter 4: Marketing Research. For the researcher who wants to maintain a competitive advantage, this chapter highlights the latest market research technologies and data gathering techniques. Topics include: definition, importance, function, marketing information and decision-support systems, market research methods and steps, resources and databases and a special topic—privacy.

Chapter 5: Consumer Behavior. In order to formulate a successful marketing strategy one must completely and thoroughly understand consumers' perceptions, motivations and evaluations. Topics include: consumer market trends, consumer decision making, internal/psychological influences, external/sociological influences, celebrity endorsements, problem-solving, adoption processes and business market buyer behavior.

Chapter 6: Market Segmentation. Effective marketers clearly identify their customer base(s). In this chapter, you will see the methods and dimensions by which companies segment their markets and select target groups. Topics include: rationale and strategies, criteria, dimensions and techniques, consumer market segmentation and business market segmentation.

Chapter 7: The Marketing Mix. The four P's—product, place, price and promotion together define and comprise the marketing mix. This chapter illuminates the myriad ways marketers manipulate these marketplace variables. Topics include: Product—planning and development, classifications, lines, classes, branding and packaging, new product development cycle, product-mix strategies; Place—channels of distribution, distribution management and strategies, physical distribution, distribution intermediaries; Pricing—meaning, importance, objectives, policies, strategies and techniques; Promotion—marketing communication process, advertising, product positioning strategy and promotional mix.

Chapter 8: Specializations. Marketing extends beyond the product/service sectors of society. This last chapter overviews marketing's special fields and applications. Topics include: services, business-to business, retailing, e-tailing, international, social marketing, permission marketing and political marketing.

PEDAGOGICAL FEATURES

Critical Thinking Questions challenge you to form your own opinion about current topics. These questions can be used to stimulate classroom discussion or as the basis for formal assignments.

Story-specific Questions highlight important points from each story.

Short Application Assignments work well as hands-on exercises for both classroom discussion and formal assignments. Most assignments should take no more than a few hours to complete. Typical assignments include developing presentations and writing one-page memos, reports, executive summaries and articles for company newsletters.

Building Research Skills exercises allow you to expand upon what you have learned from the *New York Times'* articles and explore the unlimited resources available to enhance your understanding of current events. Typical assignments include presentations, writing essays and building Web pages.

ADDITIONAL ONLINE PEDAGOGY

Sample Exercises provide examples for you to follow in completing assignments.

Additional Readings link to more than 100 additional stories, categorized by chapter, for further research.

Case Studies are an in-depth collection of stories on specific topics such as America Online, The Life and Times of the Father of Ma Bell, The Influence Industry, Music on the Internet and Microsoft on Trial.

Book Reviews cover about 80 computer and digital technology books reviewed by the *New York Times*, listed alphabetically by author and linked to the original review.

ACKNOWLEDGMENTS

My sincere appreciation goes to co-author, Dr. Edward J. Forrest, for his prompt feedback and guidance, as well as to Dr. Leisa R. Flynn and Dr. Charles F. Hofacker for their help selecting stories and crafting the pedagogy. Special recognition for patience and understanding goes to the editors with whom I've had the opportunity to work: Dr. Brian L. Massey, Nanyang Technological University, Singapore; Rob Fixmer and John Haskins, the *New York Times*; Jason Fry, the *Wall Street Journal*; Glenn Withiam, the *Cornell Hotel and Restaurant Administration Quarterly*; and Margaret Leonard, the *Florida State Times*.

This pioneering publishing project would not have been possible without the progressive thinking of the *New York Times* (Mike Levitas, Hilda Cosmo, Melanie Rosen, Christine M. Thompson, John Haskins and Jim Mones) and South-Western College Publishing (Pamela Person, Dave Shaut, Libby Shipp and Kevin von Gillern).

On a personal note, thanks to my lovely wife, Debbie, for her encouragement; my rambunctious children, Casey and Jamie, for letting me work in peace; my parents, Joan and Brannen, for their support; and my cyber-colleagues, Drs. Charles F. Hofacker, C. Edward Wotring and Edward J. Forrest for their inspiration.

CONTENTS

CHAPTER 1
The Field of Marketing — **1**

Marketers Ponder How to Sell Soap Without the Operas — 2
Saul Hansell

Schools Making Easy Money by Helping Market Research — 9
Mary B.W. Tabor

CHAPTER 2
Marketing Management — **14**

Trading on E*Trade's Success — 15
Saul Hansell

How Coke Stumbled in Handling European Contamination Scare — 21
Constance L. Hays with Alan Cowell and Craig R. Whitney

CHAPTER 3
The Marketing Environment — **27**

The Race Is On in Printer-Supply Aftermarket — 28
Claudia H. Deutsch

Microsoft Is Busy on Several Legal Fronts — 33
Lawrence M. Fisher

CHAPTER 4
Marketing Research — **39**

Whales in the Minnesota River? — 40
Tina Kelley

Net Companies Look Offline for Consumer Data — 46
Bob Tedeschi

CHAPTER 5
Consumer Behavior — 50

Online Retailers Applaud Increase in Women Shoppers — 51
Bob Tedeschi

A Sales Pitch Right Under Your Nose — 55
Kate Murphy

CHAPTER 6
Market Segmentation — 59

As Band of TV Channels Grows, Niche Programs Will Boom — 60
Lawrie Mifflin

E-Commerce Sites Target Next Generation of Buyers — 66
Bob Tedeschi

CHAPTER 7
The Marketing Mix — 70

Marketers Use Virtual Shopping To Gauge Product Potential — 72
Barnaby J. Feder

Japanese Electronics Giants Falter In U.S. Home Computer Market — 76
Steve Lohr

Direct-Pitch Stalwarts Reluctant to Sell Online — 80
Lisa Napoli

Is Coupon Clicking the Next Advertising Trend? — 86
Bob Tedeschi

CHAPTER 8
Specializations — 90

Consumers Are Critical of Online Services, Survey Finds — 92
Steve Lohr

Global Crisis for Coca-Cola, or a Pause That Refreshes? — 96
Constance L. Hays

In a Web-Centric Industry Yoyodyne Plies E-Mail — 103
Jason Chervokas and Tom Watson

From Experts to Novices, Candidates Try Campaigning Online — 107
Rebecca Fairley Raney

CHAPTER 1

The Field of Marketing

PREVIEW

Marketing is the underlying logic and force of our consumer-driven economy. Most everything you wear, eat, read, watch, listen to, drive in, ride on, try and buy is marketed. Arguably, marketing occurs any time one party (person or organization) strives to exchange something of value to another party. Marketing also extends beyond goods and services. Getting you to buy a particular brand of soap essentially is no different than getting you to donate blood.

Throughout the past century, marketing has depended on the mass media, especially TV, to disseminate its promotional messages. With the advent of interactive media such as the World Wide Web, however, things seem destined to change. Saul Hansell explores marketing's use of the Web in "Marketers Ponder How to Sell Soap Without the Operas."

Regardless of the medium, cynics have said that marketing "makes people buy things they do not need, with money they do not have, to impress people they do not like." Materialism and greed are not the only charges: lung cancer from smoking famous brands of cigarettes, alcoholism, obesity and anorexia—all at one time or another have been blamed on marketing. Most marketers, however, are aware that there has to be a balance between corporate profits and the social welfare.

The question is where to draw the line. Mary B.W. Tabor illustrates in "Schools Making Easy Money by Helping Market Research" that there are no easy answers.

Marketers Ponder How to Sell Soap Without the Operas

By Saul Hansell

CINCINNATI—Mr. Whipple, where are you now?

That seemed to be the big unanswered question during two days of high-powered industry talk, as some of the most practiced dream merchants in America assembled here at the headquarters of Procter & Gamble Co. to ponder the Internet.

P&G grew to be the nation's largest consumer products company in large part by grasping the storytelling power first of radio and then of television, and by using those media to tell the company's own 30- and 60-second stories, like the constant battles of Mr. Whipple to find time to squeeze his Charmin in peace. And often those narratives were inserted into 30- and 60-minute stories of a serial genre that Procter helped create just for that purpose: the soap opera.

Whether heartwarming or annoying, these product parables worked their way into the back of shoppers' minds so that they would reach for the Charmin, or for other Procter brands like Crest or Tide, while rolling their carts down supermarket aisles.

But now that the Internet has become the first medium to actually reduce the viewership of television—and World Wide Web surfers have shown little interest in serial storytelling—Procter is trying to figure out how to sell soap without soap operas.

That is why the company convened a two-day "summit" meeting that brought together some 400 top executives from Internet and consumer marketing companies, including America Online and Agency.com, Coca-Cola and Sears, and even Procter archrivals like Unilever and Philip Morris' Kraft Foods unit.

While much of the discussion centered on technical matters, participants struggled with issues like whether Web sites, so-called banner advertisements and other online vehicles can ever achieve the emotional resonance of a little boy in a Crest television commercial bounding up to say "Look, Ma! No cavities!"

"I can't think of one slogan developed on the Net that everybody knows," says Seth Godin, the chief executive of Yoyodyne, an Internet promotion company. "It's not a medium for the Great Big Idea."

Many of the Internet executives who attended the meeting argued that P&G, in fact, was asking the wrong question. The Internet, these experts said, might not be so much about mass-market brand building as about providing detailed information about brands consumers already recognize from other media, the way Ford Motor does with its automobiles, or for selling things directly, as Amazon.com does with books.

Marketers Ponder How to Sell Soap Without the Operas
Saul Hansell

Though often vaunted as the first medium that enables marketers to interact with consumers one to one, the Web has yet to reveal itself as a means for mass marketing the communal dreams in which a box of detergent or a can of soda comes to symbolize a way of life.

Part of the problem may be the current limitations in bandwidth, or network carrying capacity, that make the Web better suited to text, still images or simple animation than high-fidelity sound and full-motion video.

John Sculley, the former president of Pepsico and former chief executive of Apple Computer, who is now an investor in various Web-related ventures, said in a recent interview that today's Internet simply cannot be used to create the sort of hip imagery employed by Pepsi in the early 1960s and '70s.

"When we created the Pepsi Generation, we needed to make Pepsi a drink that says something about the people who drank it," Sculley said. "The Web isn't ready for that emotion yet."

Yet Procter and others insist that they can, indeed must, find ways to use the Internet to peddle packaged goods like dishwashing liquid, diapers and soap—items that might fall into the purgatory of who-cares commodities, without marketing's holy trinity of product differentiation, brand recognition and unique selling proposition.

Right now, many Web sites for consumer products emphasize information—like recipes or health facts—rather than the emotive aura that is favored by many television commercials. But one of P&G's goals for the summit meeting was to press reluctant Internet companies to offer bigger, more elaborate advertisements that can pull in the audience the way the best television commercials can.

At the same time, the company and others contend that the Internet may prove to be a catalyst for a broader change—away from a focus on products and toward services and experiences better suited to delivery online than via any other medium.

So far, P&G and other consumer product companies have been doubtful enough of the payoff to have contributed only a small fraction of the nearly $1 billion spent for online advertising last year. The Internet, for example, represents only 0.4 percent of Procter's $3 billion annual advertising budget. Unable to measure any discernible sales attributable to their initial Internet efforts, consumer product companies have so far shown themselves unwilling to spend more.

Most online advertising today takes the form of banner ads—the wide, shallow rectangles often seen at the top or bottom of Web pages, which if clicked with a mouse take the user to the advertiser's Web site. But these banners were widely disparaged at the P&G summit meeting as being too small, too ineffectual and simply too easy to ignore, to perform the hard work of building brands and selling products.

Evan Neufeld, an analyst with the research firm Jupiter Communications, presented data at the conference that underscored these concerns. In a Jupiter survey, 21 percent of Internet users polled said they never clicked on banner ads and another 51 percent said they clicked only rarely.

Such doubts notwithstanding, some big packaged-goods companies have decided that they should take a leap of faith by stepping up their online efforts. For example, Unilever, the company behind brands like Popsicle, Lipton and Ragu, has signed a deal with America Online that calls for experiments ranging from banner ads to the creation of new online areas devoted to food, health, cleaning and grooming.

"It appears you can sell automobiles and books online, but I don't know if it will be a good place to sell detergent," Richard Goldstein, head of the North American unit of Unilever, a British-Dutch company, said in an interview. Still, "you can't sit back and wait to see what happens," Goldstein added. "You have to get involved and experiment."

Unilever's Ragu spaghetti sauce was an Internet pioneer in 1995 when it set up Eat.com, a tongue-in-cheek site about Italian cooking and culture, labeled Mama's Cucina, which Unilever's Lipton Inc. food unit has continued to update.

Procter & Gamble, meanwhile, has put most of its online marketing budget behind brands like Always panty liners, Tampax tampons, Pampers diapers, Cover Girl makeup and Olean fat substitute. (So far, there is no Charmin.com.)

"Those have a narrow target audience with a more personal subject matter," said Denis Beausejour, P&G's vice president for advertising.

The company, for example, has turned Pampers.com into the Pampers Parenting Institute, addressing various issues of concern to new or expectant parents. And it is by no means the dry reference library it might appear to be at first glance.

"Our site lets a woman who is pregnant explore what will happen to her in private, so she doesn't have to ask stupid questions," Beausejour said. "That's as emotional as you can get in that context."

Some companies have tried to put entertainment on their sites to attract wired children and teen-agers. Unilever's Popsicle.com site offers games, and Warner-Lambert's Certs.com site enables users to send electronic greeting cards to people with whom they want to get cozy.

But what about products with even less emotive potential than breath mints?

"There really is a big challenge with selling soap on the Internet," said Rex Briggs, vice president of Millward Brown Interactive, a company that tests the effectiveness of advertising. "Right now the brands that do well are those that the consumer is already pretty interested in. There isn't a lot of excitement surfing a site about shampoo."

Indeed, it is because some products are so inherently unexciting that Procter has been so insistent that Internet publishers allow it to offer more attention-getting advertising. The company and other advertisers would like to see bigger ads than the standard banner—especially those called "interstitials,"

ADS FOR A WEB GENERATION

As the Internet, particularly the World Wide Web, has become a more important source of information and entertainment, advertisers have been trying to figure out how to use it to reach consumers. The search has led to the development of several categories of interactive advertisements, as well as an attempt to create some technical standards. Here is a guide to advertising on the Web.

Banner ads—These are the most common, and simplest type of ads. Guidelines for ad sizes were developed several years ago by the Coalition for Advertising Supported Information and Entertainment and the Internet Advertising Bureau, two groups supported by the advertising industry. The standards are voluntary, but most advertisers follow them. Sizes are measured in pixels, the smallest individual picture elements on a computer screen.

Interstitial ads—When someone is trying to go to a Web site, these ads will flash in the browser window for several seconds before the site is loaded. Clicking on the ad takes users to the advertiser's site.

Pop-up ads—These are very similar to interstitial ads, but instead of appearing before a Web site is loaded, a pop-up ad opens a new browser window with the advertiser's message in it. To get back to the destination Web site it is necessary to close the pop-up window.

Transactional ads—A new and increasingly popular type of ad. Instead of asking users to go to the advertiser's Web page, these ads let users request information or buy something without leaving the Web page on which the ad appears.

Rich media ads—These are not really a type of ad as much as a description of how the ads are designed. "Rich media" refers to ads that move, talk, beep or flash. Banner ads, interstitial ads, pop-up ads and transactional ads all can be rich media ads. As communication lines improve and transmission speed becomes less of an issue, these type of ads are becoming more popular.

which are screens that pop up to interrupt Web surfing the same way television ads are inserted into breaks in programming.

And Procter wants more sites to accommodate advertisements that use techniques known as "rich media," which can enable both banners and bigger ads to include animation, sound and even full video.

IPSOS/ASI, another research firm, released a study at the conference indicating that larger, more complex types of advertising are remembered more and are more likely to prompt users to click on them. Many Internet publishers, however, complain that interruptions by interstitials and the surfing slowdowns caused by rich-media ads will scare off their audiences.

"The basic methodology of advertising since I've been alive has been breaking and entering," said Meyer Berlow, the head of sales for America Online. "I jump in front of you, amuse you a little, give you a piece of information I hope will change your behavior."

But "that's a brain-dead model," Berlow said of the in-your-face approach. "It worked when there were only three channels and the bathroom. Now the consumer has a million choices."

For packaged-goods companies, like all manufacturers, the capabilities of the Web raise the question of whether they will start selling goods directly to customers rather than, as they now typically do, indirectly through wholesalers and retailers. While big-ticket items like computers or cars, or even less costly products like books, may be conducive to direct sales, the cost of packing and shipping a single tube of toothpaste or a lone jar of spaghetti sauce makes direct sales of individual items impractical.

"I'd be hard pressed to see the potential of selling our products to consumers one to one," Goldstein of Unilever said.

Of course, there are a number of companies, led by Peapod and Netgrocer, that are seeking to replace conventional supermarkets by taking online orders for a full load of groceries and shipping them to consumers. For the packaged-goods companies, the aim would be to continue making their brands the ones consumers place in their virtual shopping carts.

Unilever, for example, has struck a deal with Netgrocer to use pop-up ads to promote its products as people shop online, much as Unilever works with supermarket chains to create in-store promotions.

In the same way that demographic shifts and the rise of the female work force has changed the audience for daytime television soap operas, the Internet is a medium affected by and reflecting societal trends. In the case of the Web, this may mean less emphasis by packaged-goods purveyors on individual products and greater attention to service.

Goldstein says, for instance, that the average household now spends an average of 20 minutes a day shopping for and preparing dinner—down from two and a half hours 30 years ago. That may require food combines to sell not mere food but "meal solutions," which may include a package of ready-to-assemble ingredients supported by online information and help.

Procter & Gamble is looking at using the Internet to sell products with far more variations than could be sold through traditional supermarket chains. It has already designed an online ordering system for its Millstone premium coffee brand, for example, that lets consumers create their own blends, which are then shipped to them monthly.

"We can ask you 20 or 25 questions and blend a blend of Millstone that you

Marketers Ponder How to Sell Soap Without the Operas
Saul Hansell

will find vastly superior to the coffee you drink today," Beausejour said. "We can do things on the Internet that are not possible today in a big scale."

The New York Times, August 24, 1998
http://www.nytimes.com/library/tech/98/08/biztech/articles/24advertising.html

CRITICAL THINKING QUESTIONS

1. How could Web sites, so-called "banner" advertisements and other online marketing vehicles achieve the same emotional effects as do today's high-powered television advertisements?
2. While hailed as a "one-to-one" communication medium, how, if at all, could the Web be used effectively as a mass-marketing medium?
3. Since Internet users tend to watch less television, how could this influence marketing efforts and expenditures?
4. How can Web sites market low-involvement goods, like dishwashing liquid, diapers and soap, without using marketing's sacred trio of product differentiation, brand recognition and unique selling proposition?

STORY-SPECIFIC QUESTIONS

1. Who attended the Procter & Gamble conference? Why? What were their goals?
2. How are most Web sites used to market consumer products?
3. Briefly explain at least three common forms of online advertising.

SHORT APPLICATION ASSIGNMENTS

1. In teams or individually, answer the story-specific questions; keep your answers to 25–75 words for each question.
2. In teams of three to five persons, or as a whole class, discuss your responses to the critical thinking questions.
3. Prepare a one-page memo report (200–250 words) to your instructor in which you summarize this article. You will find a model one-page report on the Web site (nytimes.swcollege.com).
4. Write an executive summary (200–250 words). As an administrative assistant to a busy executive, you are expected to summarize selected articles and present important points. You will find a model executive summary on the Web site.
5. Summarize this article (100–125 words) for your company's newsletter. You will find a model newsletter article on the Web site.
6. In teams of three to five persons, or as a whole class, discuss how a Web site should ideally be designed to market a "low-involvement" commodity. Your instructor may assign you a specific commodity. You may also be asked to report your results in a five-minute presentation or in a one-page memo.

Chapter 1
The Field of Marketing

BUILDING RESEARCH SKILLS

1. Individually or in teams, draft a Web-marketing strategy for a specific company or product. Your instructor may give you a sample company or product. Your instructor also may ask you to submit a three- to five-page marketing strategy or post a Web page, along with a letter of transmittal explaining the project.
2. Individually or in teams, analyze three consumer-product Web sites. Your instructor may give you a sample company or product. You may also be asked to submit a three- to five-page paper or post a Web page summarizing your findings. Here are some areas to consider in your analysis: How does each site market its product or products? Are the sites used for "one-to-one" communication or for mass communication? As a consumer, which aspects of the site appeal to you and which ones do not appeal to you?
3. Using at least three other references (e.g., books, research-journal articles, newspaper or magazine stories or credible Web sites), write an 800- to 1,000-word essay addressing two of the critical thinking questions offered earlier. Assume that your essay will be used as an internal reference for a corporation's marketing plan.
4. Using at least three other references (e.g., books, research-journal articles, newspaper or magazine stories or credible Web sites), post an 800- to 1,000-word Web page addressing at least two of the earlier critical thinking questions. Assume that your page will be posted in the marketing section of a corporate intranet.

Schools Making Easy Money by Helping Market Research

By Mary B.W. Tabor

MONTCLAIR, N.J.—During recess one recent morning, 35 second graders squirmed with glee in the Watchung School auditorium at the prospect of receiving their own disposable cameras and a creative assignment: recording their lives and tastes through photographs and words.

The homework—filling out a 27-page booklet called "My All About Me Journal"—was not handed out by teachers at this public elementary school in the New York suburbs. Instead, the assignment, given to some 250 Watchung students, came from researchers for Noggin, a new educational cable television channel that forged a special partnership with the school earlier this year.

In exchange for $7,100, which the school has put toward buying 30 classroom word processors, Noggin can go into the school one morning a week from January until June to run 30-minute focus groups with students.

The researchers may also observe the children in class or have them do an assignment. The purpose, in the words of one Noggin researcher, is to find out "what sparks kids these days."

While there is nothing new about partnerships between schools looking for money and businesses looking to corner the youth market, companies like Noggin have taken the relationship to a new level, using children as captive, if willing, subjects of market research during the school day.

Hard numbers do not exist, but product research companies and advertising agencies say they have signed up dozens of schools in the past few years.

Some critics think focus groups, which for years have been conducted after school, are out of place during the school day. But the partnerships are proliferating nonetheless.

At Cumberland Elementary School in Lansing, Mich., students have taken time, occasionally class time, to participate in several focus groups in each of the last four years. The students took taste tests and answered opinion polls, earning from $2,000 to $4,000 a year for the school.

St. Joseph's, a Roman Catholic elementary school in Shawnee Mission, Kan., has received about $1,000 this year for allowing students to take part in Internet panels in which they answer questions over the school computer. The school uses the money for extras like ice cream parties or the petty-cash fund.

And in Lynnfield, Mass., students at Our Lady of Assumption elementary school spent two days last week taste testing cereal and answering an opinion poll that included questions about where they got their news (Television? Radio? Their parents?) and what television shows they liked.

The principal, Martha Marie Pooler, compared the cereal taste test, for which the school received $600, to conducting a science-class experiment.

"It's a learning experience," she said. "They had to read, they had to look, they had to compare."

For the most part, the partners to these deals—companies, school officials, teachers, parents and children—are happy with them.

"Our budget has been very tight in the past few years," said Rita Miragliotta, the Watchung School principal, who sought parent and teacher approval before accepting Noggin's offer.

"If we want extras, we have to be creative about ways to raise money. And the children really seem to enjoy it."

Like the heads of other schools doing focus groups, Mrs. Miragliotta says the deal with Noggin has been a boon. The new channel, a joint venture of Nickelodeon and the Children's Television Workshop, is a 24-hour, commercial-free educational channel whose revenues come from subscriptions.

The Watchung students usually participate at recess. And the children, Mrs. Miragliotta said, are learning some analytical thinking—and even computer skills.

Focus groups in schools are just one instance of the growing corporate presence in public and private education. In recent years, about 100 school districts have accepted profit-making companies as sponsors or advertisers, according to the Education Commission of the States, a nonprofit group based in Denver that studies education issues.

The Eanes Independent School District in Austin, Tex., sold exclusive vending rights to Coca-Cola for $350,000 a year. For selling similar rights to Pepsico, the Jefferson County School District near Denver received $2.1 million over seven years, plus $48,000 a year in scholarships. And New York City and Colorado Springs now sell advertising space on school buses.

"There is an increased level of sophistication with how corporations are approaching schools," said the development director of a New York City private school, who spoke on the condition that he not be named out of concern that he would jeopardize potential partnerships.

The idea of paid polling in school is raising some criticism, even among those who consider focus groups less offensive than outright marketing to children.

"It seems to me that there should be some places left, like school, where the kids are not targeted," said Marcie Wyant, a consumer-science teacher at the Boynton Middle School in Ithaca, N.Y., and one of a growing number of teachers who try to make students aware of consumerism, commercialism and media literacy. "Focus groups just shouldn't be done during taxpayer time."

David Walsh, president of the National Institute of Media and the Family, a nonprofit group based in Minnesota, agreed. "Whenever we cross the line of allowing commercial enterprises to do their work during the school day on school time, I think it raises questions," he said. "The challenge here is, where do you draw the line?"

In October, the National Association of State Boards of Education tried to draw the line by passing a set of principles to help guide schools as they enter such partnerships. One of the eight principles is: "Selling or providing access to a captive audience in the classroom for commercial purposes is exploitation and a violation of the public trust."

State boards are free to set their own policies, and some did with the advent of Channel One, a company that provides free televisions and broadcasts programs—and commercials—in classrooms. Many school officials said they were not aware of the national association's guidelines.

Meanwhile, it has dawned on product researchers that schools are an ideal place to do their work.

"It all goes back to the realization in the corporate sector that the education marketplace offers tremendous potential to sell products and to gain access to the youth market, and through that to the adult market," said Robert Reynolds, president of Education Market Resources, a research company founded six years ago and based in Kansas that matches schools with corporate research projects.

Its clients include the Kentucky Fried Chicken Corporation, the Kellogg Company and Nabisco Inc.

Reynolds took care to distinguish between the companies themselves and the firms that do research for them.

"Most companies to this day do not think they can go into schools, and in most cases they cannot," he said. "If McDonald's was to approach schools, a lot of people would perceive them as exploiting the children."

The researchers convert their work into "an educational process" for the children, Reynolds said, and they do not mention which companies they are doing research for. In one recent project for Nike, he said, his researchers gave children disposable cameras and asked them to take pictures of their favorite place to hang out.

"Kids these days love the feeling of empowerment," he said. "And we are empowering them, but we are doing it in a proper way."

Kathleen Lalley, a planning director at the Leo Burnett Company, an advertising agency based in Chicago, said her agency had also begun running focus groups inside schools in recent years. Less than a year ago, Ms. Lalley said, the company created a special unit, called Kidleo, to focus on marketing for children.

At Watchung School about half the parents did not sign permission slips, so their children do not participate in the market research. A handful of those parents said they did not approve of the program, and one wrote Mrs. Miragliotta to protest.

That parent, John C. Fisher, called the focus groups blatant commercialism.

"I think it's exploitative," Fisher said. He is a vice president at HBO

Downtown Productions, whose parent company, Time Warner Inc., competes with Nickelodeon's parent, Viacom Inc. Partly because of that potential conflict, Fisher would not allow his children to take part in the research. But also, he said, "I don't think this is appropriate."

Susan J. Stohr, head of Watchung's School Review, a parent advisory board, said that so far, the Noggin partnership had been a positive experience. "I would be very cautious of anything that took away from curriculum time," said Ms. Stohr, who has two children at the school. "But this really hasn't. Beyond that, I think exposure to this type of thing can be very positive."

One of the students participating, Katherine Carpenter, 7, said she thought the Noggin projects "look fun."

And Noggin executives said that their mission was simply to do research to provide a better, more appealing educational channel for children.

"We want to have programming that is highly appropriate for children," said Tom Ascheim, general manager of Noggin. "Our mission is to serve kids' natural urge to learn. And we want to do that by creating a place where learning is driven by them."

The New York Times, April 5, 1999
http://www.nytimes.com/library/national/040599educ-partners.html

CRITICAL THINKING QUESTIONS

1. How—if at all—should schools and organizations decide between profiting from the privacy rights of their students, employees or citizens, as opposed to protecting those rights?
2. What are some ways in which schools and organizations are profiting from information about their students, employees or citizens? Why do you condone or not condone the specific examples you name?
3. What are some ways in which schools and organizations are profiting by providing marketers with access to a "captive audience" of students, employees or citizens? Why do you condone or not condone the specific examples you name?
4. What are the arguments for and against the idea of marketers working with schools and organizations?

STORY-SPECIFIC QUESTIONS

1. What were the specific arrangements between Wachtung School and Noggin?
2. What are three other examples of arrangements between schools and marketers?

SHORT APPLICATION ASSIGNMENTS

1. In teams or individually, answer the story-specific questions; keep your answers to 25–75 words for each question.

2. In teams of three to five persons, or as a whole class, discuss your responses to the critical thinking questions.
3. Prepare a one-page memo report (200–250 words) to your instructor in which you summarize this article. You will find a model one-page report on the Web site (nytimes.swcollege.com).
4. Write an executive summary (200–250 words). As an administrative assistant to a busy executive, you are expected to summarize selected articles and present important points. You will find a model executive summary on the Web site.
5. Summarize this article (100–125 words) for your company's newsletter. You will find a model newsletter article on the Web site.
6. In teams of three to five persons, or as a whole class, discuss your school's dealings with corporate marketing. Your instructor may assign you a specific corporation. You may also be asked to report your results in a five-minute presentation or in a one-page memo.

BUILDING RESEARCH SKILLS

1. Individually or in teams, draft a marketing partnership policy for your school that addresses privacy and captive-audience concerns. Your instructor may give you a sample school. You may also be asked to submit a three- to five-page policy handbook or post a Web page, along with a letter of transmittal explaining the project.
2. Individually or in teams, analyze a school's marketing partnerships. Your instructor may give you a sample school. You may also be asked to submit a three- to five-page paper or post a Web page summarizing your findings. Here are some areas to consider in your analysis: How many different ways is privacy breached or captive audiences marketed to? Who is doing that marketing? As a school member, what seems fair to you and what does not seem fair to you?
3. Using at least three other references (e.g., books, research-journal articles, newspaper or magazine stories or credible Web sites), write an 800- to 1,000-word essay addressing two of the critical thinking questions offered earlier. Assume that your essay will be used as an internal reference for a school's marketing plan.
4. Using at least three other references (e.g., books, research-journal articles, newspaper or magazine stories or credible Web sites), post an 800- to 1,000-word Web page addressing at least two of the earlier critical thinking questions. Assume that your page will be posted in the policy section of a corporate intranet.

CHAPTER 2

Marketing Management

PREVIEW

Marketing management plans, directs and controls the marketing activities of an organization.

First, *strategic marketing planning* identifies opportunities, determines an appropriate marketing mix (product, place, promotion and price) to satisfy the needs of a selected target market(s), and allocates resources to achieve marketing goals.

Next, based on the identified opportunities, the marketing manager develops a *marketing strategy* that is aimed at producing a *competitive advantage* that is sustainable, profitable and not easily duplicated by competitors.

Normally a time-consuming and deliberate process, Christos Cotsakos of E*Trade puts strategic marketing planning on Internet time, leading what Cotsakos says is a revolution turning into a movement. In "Trading on E*Trade's Success," Saul Hansell examines E*Trade's wide-ranging and aggressive online trading initiatives.

No matter the depth of strategic planning, the best-laid plans sometimes fail. Unexpected events happen. *Crisis management* attempts to minimize the effects of unfavorable publicity or unexpected unfavorable events. Constance L. Hays, Alan Cowell and Craig R. Whitney explore Coca-Cola's crisis management of the biggest product recall in the company's 113-year history in "How Coke Stumbled in Handling European Contamination Scare."

Trading on E*Trade's Success

By Saul Hansell

If a computer glitch kept thousands of customers unsatisfied, wouldn't any company be embarrassed?

Not E*Trade, the brash Internet stock brokerage company. It ended its shareholder meeting last week with an elaborate video montage of the news coverage of its three days of trading halts in February. While Christos M. Cotsakos, the company's chief executive, acknowledged that E*Trade had to prevent such problems from recurring, he used the video mainly as a rousing affirmation of E*Trade's success.

"Other companies have had systems issues, but we were the only company to get worldwide coverage in virtually every media," Cotsakos said in an interview last week. "The degree to which we have been recognized as a leader in this space is unequaled. And that is something we should be very proud of."

That is typical bravado from Cotsakos, who likes to say he is not simply running a company but rather leading a "revolution that is turning into a movement" as online trading grows to account for one in every seven stock trades in the country.

Now, Cotsakos wants his revolutionaries to charge from the stock exchange to the shopping mall and the television station. E*Trade, he said, is becoming a "digital financial media company" that will offer financial transactions, information, advertising and electronic shopping over the Internet, cable television and even wireless hand-held devices.

In effect, he wants to marry the media aspirations of Internet portals like Yahoo! with the dream of building a financial supermarket. Oh, yes, Cotsakos also wants E*Trade to foment this movement in more than 30 countries.

Yet by fighting on so many fronts, Cotsakos risks giving up the ground that E*Trade has already won in the brokerage business, where competition from Charles Schwab, Fidelity and Merrill Lynch is growing more intense. He has even sacrificed E*Trade's position as one of the few profitable Internet companies in order to spend as much as $150 million on an extravagant marketing blitz meant to attract a million new customers during the next year.

"Christos has the most expansive vision of what an online trading company can become," said Bill Burnham, an analyst with Credit Suisse First Boston. "But that kind of aggressive attitude, being willing to try stuff that other people don't think is completely baked, is a double-edged sword. They could be throwing money down a black hole."

Investors certainly found the timing of the marketing plan half-baked. It was announced last summer just as a market slump raised fears that volume at stockbrokers would dry up. E*Trade's shares fell to $6 in October, adjusted for a recent 2-for-1 split, from $17.25 in August.

Cotsakos readily acknowledges he has had some selling to do, but that is what he is good at.

"If you are making money, how do you convince shareholders that by losing money you will increase value in the long run?" Cotsakos asked in an earlier interview. "With absolute, sheer fundamentalist dedication, I said the only way we would be successful was to take big bold risks and to move very quickly."

Now the company's stock has bounced back, buoyed by the surging market and some early positive return on the marketing campaign. The shares closed Monday at $54.125, giving E*Trade a market value of $6.2 billion—now larger than that of Paine Webber, a more conventional brokerage firm. Perhaps more important, investors have come to realize that Cotsakos' plan to lose lots of money to finance rapid growth resembles the strategy of highly valued Internet companies like Amazon.com.

"Christos has turned E*Trade from a brokerage play to an Internet play," noted Julio Gomez, who runs a consulting firm focused on electronic trading.

Not all investors are convinced.

"Christos rubs institutional investors one of two ways," Burnham, the First Boston analyst said. "Some are caught up in the vision. Others are turned off and say he's a self-promoter who doesn't know anything about the blocking and tackling of the brokerage business."

Still, even some competitors acknowledge that so far E*Trade has been able to deliver on most of its grandiose promises.

"They have thrown the long pass, and then to my surprise, they have run forward to catch it every time," said the head of a major online brokerage operation who spoke on condition of anonymity.

When Cotsakos, 50, joined E*Trade just before its initial public offering in 1996, he knew nothing of Wall Street. But he brought a passionate leadership style, built on his experience as an Army squad leader in Vietnam and honed by his failure to make it as an actor.

After his acting career stumbled, he signed on as a $3-an-hour package handler at Federal Express. He worked his way up rapidly and was assigned to run the company's operations in Continental Europe in 1988.

In 1992, he was hired to run the European operations of A.C. Nielsen, the big market research company. He rose to become president but left the company just before its owner, Dun & Bradstreet, took it public.

"Nielsen was not successful when Cotsakos was there," said James D. Dougherty, an analyst with Paine Webber who has long followed the company. "He banked all the company's future on whiz-bang silver-bullet software that just never worked." (Cotsakos said Dun & Bradstreet would not invest the money needed to realize his plans.)

At E*Trade Group, based in Palo Alto, Calif., Cotsakos draws from both his military and theatrical experience to practice what one employee calls "management by revival meeting." He eschews formal meetings for what he calls

Trading on E*Trade's Success
Saul Hansell

"swarms," more informal sessions in which employees buzz briefly about dealing with a problem. And he will surprise his executives with sudden changes in strategy, such as replacing E*Trade's somber gold-and-black logo last year with a hip and decidedly unfinancial green and purple model.

"He will take your breath away," said Lisa Nash, a vice president for marketing. "That's part of his management style."

Cotsakos hired a management team drawn largely from outside financial services, and they have brought some unconventional ideas. Debra J. Chrapaty, who was recruited from the National Basketball Association, has built a computer system based on a network of dozens of small workstation computers—unusual in finance services, which typically relies on mainframes to keep customer data secure.

The company's marketing is in the hands of Jerry Gramaglia, who was recruited from Sprint. Last week, he hired Omnicom Group's Goodby, Silverstein & Partners, the advertising agency that produced the "Got milk?" campaign, to create a successor to E*Trade's long-running "Someday we'll all invest this way" campaign.

That campaign began when E*Trade's $20 commission level differentiated it from its more expensive competitors. But now competitors like Fidelity and Schwab have lowered their prices. And deep discounters have emerged, like Datek and Ameritrade, with commissions under $10.

Full-service firms like Morgan Stanley Dean Witter, Donaldson Lufkin & Jenrette and Merrill Lynch, meanwhile, are offering research and advice along with online trading. And Schwab, which has become the leading online broker despite $30 commissions, is devoting considerable effort to offering advice and hand-holding to lure customers from firms like Merrill.

E*Trade does not fear being caught in the middle as the leader in neither price nor service.

"Schwab's position is that most people who come online are clueless and need a broker as a security blanket," Gramaglia said. "That is not whom we target. We believe that most customers are smart enough and capable enough to control their own investments once we give them the same tools that brokers have."

An expanded tool kit is the centerpiece of the company's expensive new strategy: Destination E*Trade. It has refashioned its Internet site to offer casual visitors as well as customers all sorts of up-to-the-minute information, research, bulletin boards and other investing tools, at a cost to E*Trade of several dollars a month for each "member." It is modeled on the popular finance channels of Yahoo! and the other portals, where E*Trade was advertising at ever increasing prices.

"We were being held hostage to someone else's distribution channel," Cotsakos said. "It was getting very costly if you didn't own your own distribution."

The results from E*Trade's refurbished Web site have so far been mixed. In the last three months of 1998, E*Trade spent $41 million in marketing, including the cost of the site, TV commercials and inducements like $50 rebates for people who opened accounts. That has brought in 500,000 members and 97,000 new brokerage accounts (excluding the low-margin corporate options business), according to Burnham, the First Boston analyst.

That works out to a cost of $404 to lure each new core brokerage account. Since Burnham estimates that the average account will produce only $526 in profits over the life of the customer, E*Trade may have little to show for its efforts.

E*Trade, however, says it can make two or three times that by finding other ways to profit from an affluent customer base. It will expand its own site with banking, mutual funds and other services. And it will sell advertising and generate commissions from referring customers to other online merchants.

So far, the move into advertising has been disappointing, Cotsakos acknowledges, bringing in less than $200,000 in the most recent quarter. But he argues that ad revenue will grow quickly, now that the company has expanded its sales force.

Cotsakos also wants to offer a greater range of products to corporations and institutions. The company has invested in E*Offering, an investment bank backed by Sanford Robertson, to compete with Wall Street investment bankers in initial public offerings. And it plans to attract big institutional investors with a service combining electronic stock trading with the sort of data provided by Reuters and Bloomberg.

E*Trade has also franchised its name and its systems for use by brokerage firms in 33 countries. Currently, its affiliates have opened in Canada and Australia. The company expects Britain, Japan and a few others to follow this year.

It took six months and a revived but still wobbly market in Internet stocks for E*Trade to regain the confidence of investors. But Cotsakos promises even more changes.

"We will morph again in a year," he said. It will start a new "asterisk channel" after E*Trade's logo, that is a combination of CNBC and a sort of financial home shopping network.

"To me, the game from here is about interactive multimedia. It's not the Internet. It's how you take the convergence of video, voice and data on wireless phones, computers and television to give people what they want."

For E*Trade, however, to be any more than an asterisk in the history of finance, investors and analysts say it will also have pay attention to the basics, making sure that last month's computer problems do not happen regularly again.

"I'm impressed by the breadth of stuff they are talking about doing," said Burnham, "But I hope that someone remembers to complete the trades."

The New York Times, March 16, 1999
http://www.nytimes.com/library/tech/99/03/biztech/articles/16etrade-marketplace.html

CRITICAL THINKING QUESTIONS

1. How might online trading grow and evolve over the next few years?
2. Why do you agree or disagree with Cotsakos' vision for online trading?
3. What strategic marketing planning advice would you offer traditional brokers such as Merrill Lynch, Morgan Stanley, Dean Witter or Fidelity Investments?

STORY-SPECIFIC QUESTIONS

1. Based on Cotsakos' plans, write a "mission statement" for E*Trade.
2. Based on Cotsakos' plans, write three marketing objectives for E*Trade.
3. What are the advantages and disadvantages of Cotsakos' aggressive plans for E*Trade?

SHORT APPLICATION ASSIGNMENTS

1. In teams or individually, answer the story-specific questions; keep your answers to 25–75 words for each question.
2. In teams of three to five persons, or as a whole class, discuss your responses to the critical thinking questions.
3. Prepare a one-page memo report (200–250 words) to your instructor in which you summarize this article. You will find a model one-page report on the Web site (nytimes.swcollege.com).
4. Write an executive summary (200–250 words). As an administrative assistant to a busy executive, you are expected to summarize selected articles and present important points. You will find a model executive summary on the Web site.
5. Summarize this article (100–125 words) for your company's newsletter. You will find a model newsletter article on the Web site.
6. In teams of three to five persons, or as a whole class, discuss how a financial Web site should ideally be designed. Your instructor may assign you a specific financial company. You may also be asked to report your results in a five-minute presentation or in a one-page memo.
7. In teams of three to five persons, or as a whole class, discuss the key elements in a marketing plan for E*Trade. You may also be asked to report your results in a five-minute presentation or in a one-page memo.

BUILDING RESEARCH SKILLS

1. Individually or in teams, draft a marketing plan for a specific financial company. Your instructor may give you a sample company. You may also be asked to submit a three- to five-page marketing plan or post a Web page, along with a letter of transmittal explaining the marketing plan.
2. Individually or in teams, analyze three financial Web sites. Your instructor may give you a sample company. You may also be asked to submit a three- to five-page paper

or post a Web page summarizing your findings. Here are some areas to consider in your analysis: How does each site market its products and/or services? As a consumer, what appeals to you about the site and what about it does not appeal to you?

3. Using at least three other references (e.g., books, research-journal articles, newspaper or magazine stories or credible Web sites), write an 800- to 1,000-word essay addressing two of the critical thinking questions offered earlier. Assume that your essay will be used as an internal reference for a corporation's marketing plan.

4. Using at least three other references (e.g., books, research-journal articles, newspaper or magazine stories or credible Web sites), post an 800- to 1,000-word Web page addressing at least two of the earlier critical thinking questions. Assume that your page will be posted in the marketing section of a corporate intranet.

How Coke Stumbled in Handling European Contamination Scare

By Constance L. Hays with Alan Cowell and Craig R. Whitney

As Coca-Cola Co. tries to regain its footing in Europe after a contamination scare that caused the biggest product recall in the company's 113-year history, executives have made a rare admission: that mistakes were made in manufacturing.

Such humility is far from routine for the soft-drink giant, renowned as it is for superb marketing and a corporate structure that is well-oiled from top to bottom. But the crisis in Europe, in which hundreds of people said they felt sick after drinking Cokes, has revealed a different Coca-Cola, one that stumbled repeatedly, making an unfortunate situation even worse.

When the outbreak began, Coke executives took several days to make the matter a high priority. An apology to consumers came more than a week after the first public reports that people had fallen ill. It was not until June 18–10 days after the first schoolboy became dizzy and nauseated after drinking a Coke—that top company officials arrived in Belgium. And when Coke did begin to respond, it attempted to minimize the reports of illness.

"I am genuinely amazed that they have reacted like this, and I don't know what has gone on inside the company to make them react like this," said David Arnold, a Harvard Business School marketing professor who has studied Coke for years.

The cardinal rule of consumer-products marketing is that the customers' perceptions—often divorced from the facts—are what count, he said, adding that a company like Coke, which has built an $18.8 billion business out of sugar water, should know that better than anyone. "They should have said yes, there appears to be a problem, instead of arguing the facts," he said.

It will be weeks before the damage to Coca-Cola can be fully assessed. Analysts have already knocked a few pennies per share off earnings estimates for the current quarter for both Coca-Cola and Coca-Cola Enterprises, Coke's bottler in Belgium. Beyond that, it is clear that in Europe, which accounts for about 26 percent of Coca-Cola's profits, Coke must take aggressive steps to restore its image.

Philippe L'Enfant, a senior executive with Coca-Cola Enterprises, told a Belgian television station on Sunday that the company "perhaps lost control of the situation to a certain extent." While the firm had a crisis management strategy, he said, "The crisis was bigger than any worst-case scenario we could have imagined."

Coca-Cola's muted initial approach to its problems appears to have backfired. In a news conference in Brussels last week, company chairman

M. Douglas Ivester said he had chosen to "take a lower profile on this," at the request of Belgian Health Minister Luc van den Brossche, and other officials of Belgium's government.

Yet Coke had taken a low profile well before any ministers took charge. A bar owner outside Antwerp reported May 12 that four people felt sick after drinking bottles of Coke that smelled strange. That incident did not lead to public safety warnings, although samples were tested, and no mention was made of it after other incidents were reported, beginning June 8, because, a Coca-Cola spokesman said, it was unclear whether they were connected.

Government officials in Belgium and France complained repeatedly about Coca-Cola's apparent inability to tell them, in timely fashion, what it knew. "You can say that since the beginning, Coca-Cola has presented real contradictions," said one French official involved in the investigation.

Some of those contradictions were evident within Coke itself. One spokesman said this week that the May 12 incident was widely known, since it had been "extensively covered in the Belgian press." Another spokesman said minutes earlier that he had never heard of it.

When the first reports of illness were made June 8, local executives of Coca-Cola Enterprises were called in. That day, a Tuesday, schoolchildren in Bornem who had been sold Coke in 200-centiliter glass bottles by their schools experienced dizziness, nausea and other symptoms that ended with 42 of them being hospitalized over the next 24 hours.

Odilon Hermans, the director of the St. Mary school in Bornem, a well-to-do suburb of Brussels, contacted the Coca-Cola Enterprises bottling plant in Antwerp that day. He said several managers visited the school and the hospital before nightfall.

While a Belgian health official said the bottler had recalled several batches of suspect Coke on June 8, it was not until June 10 that remaining unopened bottles at the school were taken away, Hermans said. "It was after we had to push them a little bit in the beginning," he said.

The government decided to get deeply involved on June 10, after eight children from Bruges, outside Brussels, had to be hospitalized, said Susan Grognard, an assistant to van den Brossche, the Belgian Health Minister. They said they felt sick after drinking cans of Coca-Cola and Fanta, a fruit-flavored brand owned by Coke.

"From that moment, we began following it very closely," said the health official. Coke executives were summoned to van den Brossche's offices for a meeting the following day.

The meeting took place at noon. About four hours later, the ministry learned that 13 more children had been hospitalized in Harelbeke, showing the same symptoms as the children in Bruges and Bornem.

The news came at a sensitive time. Belgian elections were only two days

How Coke Stumbled in Handling European Contamination Scare

Constance L. Hays with Alan Cowell and Craig R. Whitney

away. Two ministers had already lost their jobs as a result of an earlier, unrelated scare in which animal feed contaminated with dioxin, a substance that can cause cancer, was found across Belgium.

That evening, the Belgian government informed the European Commission and French officials of the steps it had taken. The Belgians also set up a call center to field questions about Coke. It received more than 200 calls by Monday, June 14. That day, 42 children were taken to the hospital in Lochristi. Eight more were hospitalized in Korttrijk the next day.

As more reports of illness were made, the government ordered Coke to remove its products from schools. The removal was not a perfect process.

"There was a situation where there was a vending machine in a school and the building was locked, and we couldn't get to it over the weekend," said Randy Donaldson, a Coca-Cola spokesman.

On Sunday, voters removed the prime minister from office, and on Monday, the Belgian government ordered all Coke products off the market. Luxembourg enacted its own ban the next day. The government of the Netherlands banned Coke products shipped through Belgium. And health authorities in France asked Coca-Cola to shut down its plant in Dunkirk, near the Belgian border, after Coke said that a substance found on some cans shipped from Dunkirk was not normally used by the company.

Coca-Cola executives said that flawed carbon dioxide, the gas that produces the bubbles in a carbonated soft drink, probably caused the smell some of the Belgian children reported. And the substance on the cans, para-chloro-meta-cresol, was traced to wooden pallets used to transport them from the Dunkirk plant. The pallets, ordered from a Dutch company, used the solvent although it did not meet Coke's specifications, said Robert Pagani, senior vice president for operations at Coca-Cola Enterprises.

As the bans spread in Europe, Coca-Cola resolutely insisted that its products were not bad for anyone. "It may make you feel sick, but it is not harmful," said Rob Baskin, a spokesman at company headquarters in Atlanta.

On June 16, in a statement issued at 10:30 P.M. Brussels time, Ivester issued a terse apology from Atlanta. "We deeply regret any problems experienced by our European consumers," he said.

That day, German officials removed Coke products that had been bottled in France or Belgium. Consumer groups in Germany and elsewhere said the company had been less than direct and was unreassuring in its public explanations, including assertions that the drinks were safe even though people had gotten sick after consuming them.

In responding, Coca-Cola executives displayed a curious indifference to the political and social concerns in Europe, which ranged from fears of dioxin to trade squabbles over bananas, surrounding the events involving their own products. In such an atmosphere, "this would be quite scary to a consumer, because you would assume that Coca-Cola, which is a totally artificial, manufactured product, would not have any problems," Arnold said. "Meat or fruit might be a risk. But not something like Coca-Cola."

Ivester arrived in Brussels for the first time June 18. At one point that day he telephoned James Burke, the chairman of Johnson & Johnson during the Tylenol tampering crisis in the 1980s, and talked "at great length," according to Burke's assistant.

As he did so, regional health authorities in Spain were recalling thousands of cases of Coke products, and Germany warned consumers to be sure their Cokes were made in Germany, to be safe. There were no reports of illness from Germany or Spain, and none from Luxembourg or the Netherlands.

As the bans on Coke products continued into Monday, June 21, Ivester issued a memo to all of his company's 28,000 employees. The subject was the "Belgian Issue," and it said, among other things, that the company's "quality control processes in Belgium faltered." Suggesting there was no cause for alarm, he added: "I have personally tasted the products and held the packages involved with no adverse reaction."

Full-page newspaper advertisements appeared that day in French newspapers, asserting the safety of Coke products and listing a toll-free number for people to call with any safety questions.

At the same time, Coke circulated a toxicologist's report it had commissioned, which concluded that substances found in the products in question—such as hydrogen sulfide and the phenol compound—were present in amounts too small to have caused the symptoms people reported. It fanned rumors, reported in European newspapers, that people who said they got sick were actually experiencing "psychosomatic" illnesses.

Coke ran ads in Belgian newspapers June 22 that consisted of a more contrite apology, topped by a photograph of a smiling Ivester. "I should have spoken to you earlier, and I apologize for that," the ad read. "Over the past several days in Belgium, we allowed two breakdowns to occur in fulfilling the promise of Coca-Cola."

The next day, June 23, Belgium lifted the ban on Coke's bottled and canned soft drinks. Van den Brossche said Coke had agreed to conditions, including more quality control, set by him.

By Friday, all other countries had followed suit, and complaints of illness had, for the moment at least, ceased. An investigation continues in France, focused on the Dunkirk plant. Vending machines remain shut down in Belgium until the authorities check all 11,000 of them.

Tuesday the company announced a recall in Poland, this time of its Bonaqua bottled water. Mold was found growing at the bottom of 1,500 bottles, according to Coke officials, who said it was not dangerous, although Polish health officials said it could cause digestive problems.

How Coke Stumbled in Handling European Contamination Scare
Constance L. Hays with Alan Cowell and Craig R. Whitney

The New York Times, June 30, 1999
http://www.nytimes.com/library/financial/063099coke-europe.html

CRITICAL THINKING QUESTIONS

1. Overall, why did Coca-Cola handle this crisis correctly—or why did the company handle it incorrectly?
2. What general guidelines would you suggest for crisis management?
3. Given a second chance, how would you suggest that Coca-Cola should manage this crisis?
4. What, if any, will be the long-term effects of Coca-Cola's management of this crisis?

STORY-SPECIFIC QUESTIONS

1. What were three mistakes that Coca-Cola made in managing this crisis?
2. How did the various involved governments react to this crisis?

SHORT APPLICATION ASSIGNMENTS

1. In teams or individually, answer the story-specific questions; keep your answers to 25–75 words for each question.
2. In teams of three to five persons, or as a whole class, discuss your responses to the critical thinking questions.
3. Prepare a one-page memo report (200–250 words) to your instructor in which you summarize this article. You will find a model one-page report on the Web site (nytimes.swcollege.com).
4. Write an executive summary (200–250 words). As an administrative assistant to a busy executive, you are expected to summarize selected articles and present important points. You will find a model executive summary on the Web site.
5. Summarize this article (100–125 words) for your company's newsletter. You will find a model newsletter article on the Web site.
6. In teams of three to five persons, or as a whole class, discuss your school's crisis management policies. Your instructor may assign you a specific crisis to discuss. You may also be asked to report your results in a five-minute presentation or in a one-page memo.

BUILDING RESEARCH SKILLS

1. Individually or in teams, draft a crisis management policy for a school. Your instructor may give you a sample school. You may also be asked to submit a three- to five-page policy handbook or post a Web page, along with a letter of transmittal explaining the project.

Chapter 2
Marketing Management

2. Individually or in teams, analyze a school's handling of a crisis. Your instructor may give you a sample crisis. You may also be asked to submit a three- to five-page paper or post a Web page summarizing your findings.
3. Using at least three other references (e.g., books, research-journal articles, newspaper or magazine stories or credible Web sites), write an 800- to 1,000-word essay addressing two of the critical thinking questions offered earlier. Assume that this essay will be used as an internal reference for a school's crisis management plan.
4. Using at least three other references (e.g., books, research-journal articles, newspaper or magazine stories or credible Web sites), post an 800- to 1,000-word Web page addressing at least two of the earlier critical thinking questions. Assume that this page will be posted in the policy section of a corporate intranet.

CHAPTER 3

The Marketing Environment

PREVIEW

Marketing managers must constantly monitor their environments. The external environment is often referred to by two acronyms: PESTE (political, economic, social and technological environments) or SWOT (strengths, weaknesses, opportunities and threats). The internal environment includes an organization's image, production facilities, financial and human resources, location and research and development capabilities.

Based on this ongoing *environmental monitoring*, marketers are better able to adjust their marketing mix—product, price, place and promotion—for existing products. Environmental monitoring also helps businesses identify and evaluate *new marketing opportunities*.

Claudia H. Deutsch's "The Race Is On in Printer-Supply Aftermarket" exemplifies the need for environmental marketing. Economic conditions, competition, manufacturing and legal issues are a few of the environmental factors influencing the printer supply market.

Perhaps no company is more familiar with the legal environment than Microsoft. Lawrence M. Fisher describes Microsoft's non-stop legal battles in "Microsoft Is Busy on Several Legal Fronts."

Hewlett-Packard cartridges now compete with aftermarket brands in retail stores, by mail-order, and on line.

Source: Edward Keating/The New York Times

The Race Is On in Printer-Supply Aftermarket

By Claudia H. Deutsch

Xerox Corp.'s executives did not miss a shot when they met with distributors and customers last month. Sure, they talked up Xerox's new low-end printers, and its growing lines of digital copiers.

But their hottest topic wasn't any Xerox machine. It was the discount-priced replacement toner cartridges that Xerox has started making for use on Hewlett-Packard Co.'s laser printers.

"If you can provide a quality product at a lower price, why not do it?" said Larry Wash, a vice president of the Xerox Supplies Group.

He is on to something. With computer printers becoming ubiquitous in offices and homes, more companies are recognizing that there are billions of dollars to be made in keeping them inked up. They figure, let the Hewlett-Packards and such sell the machines, at razor-thin margins; the real money is in supplies.

"We can certainly make an ink that works as well as theirs," said Jim Daggs, marketing manager for General Ribbon Corp.

General Ribbon is just one of thousands of so-called aftermarket companies looking to sell replacement printer supplies. They range from mom-and-pop shops to $173 million public companies like Nashua Corp. They have for years sold cartridges, toners and inks at prices 30 percent or more below the $25 that a typical ink-jet cartridge goes for, and as little as half the $200 or more that a toner cartridge costs.

Never mind that Hewlett-Packard, which commands two-thirds of the ink-jet printer market, has patented its cartridge. The aftermarket companies refill the old cartridges, or sell the necessary inks and syringes to users. The field is open even wider for toner cartridges for laser printers, which usually can be replicated or refilled without violating patents.

The stakes are huge. Almost $5 billion worth of replacement toner cartridges and almost $6.5 billion of ink-jet cartridges will be sold this year, according to the research firm CAP Ventures Inc.

Until recently, the printer makers tolerated the interlopers. Not anymore. They are cutting prices, filing lawsuits, even tinkering with their products to make them hard to refill.

"They've realized that the biggest money is in supplies," said John Shane, a CAP Ventures consultant.

The timing is no coincidence. As competition for printer sales drives profit margins down, cartridge sales are looking ever more important.

"Hewlett has an immense interest in shielding itself from competition," said Ashish Kishore, an analyst with Credit Research and Trading.

Indeed it does. "We've got 55 million customers out there who've already

The Race Is On in Printer-Supply Aftermarket
Claudia H. Deutsch

bought our printers," said Kenneth Crangle, Hewlett-Packard's marketing manager for ink-jet supplies, "but who will keep buying cartridges."

Yes, but whose? According to CAP Ventures, aftermarket companies will this year sell more than a quarter of the replacement laser toner cartridges and 22 percent of the ink-jet cartridges.

"I don't think the big boys ever anticipated how big this market would become," said Cheryle White, executive editor of *The Cartridge Recycling Magazine*, which is published on the Internet.

But now, the aftermarket has grown large enough to attract billion-dollar players. There is Xerox, of course. NCR Corp.'s Systemedia Group just started selling printer supplies. Lexmark International, a printer maker itself, has introduced toner cartridges for Hewlett-Packard printers. Eastman Kodak Co., which makes toner for its own laser printers, is also taking a hard look at the aftermarket.

"Let's just say that we look at all supplies as a growth area," said Karel Czanderna, general manager of Kodak's supplies business.

The aftermarket's heightened appeal has myriad roots. As typewriters and impact printers fade into memories, ribbon manufacturers like NCR, Nu-Kote International and General Ribbon are turning to printer supplies to pick up the slack.

Home users, entrepreneurs and corporate procurement executives have grown more receptive to cheaper supplies of acceptable, if not totally comparable, quality.

The national push toward recycling has yielded a steady supply of spent cartridges to refill. Suppliers of parts and inks that once sold only to printer manufacturers now also supply aftermarket companies.

And, the advent of the World Wide Web, home shopping networks and other alternative marketing routes have given even tiny aftermarket companies a national reach.

"The Web let us go from a local refiller to a national supplier almost overnight," said Bart Como, the owner of Nu-Jet Inc., a San Antonio maker of ink-jet refill kits and Epson-compatible cartridges whose sales have increased tenfold, to $1 million, since it started selling through the Web in late 1995. Similarly, JR Inkjet Inc. has used its Web page and distributors it has met at computer shows to sell $2 million worth of a "universal ink" that it says can be used to refill any printer's cartridge.

While the small aftermarket companies get bigger, the big ones are getting huge. Last year, NCR bought 26 percent of Turbon International, a German company that makes toner and laser cartridges. Mark Quinlan, NCR Systemedia's vice president for global marketing, says both companies are running at capacity. "We figured our revenues would grow 30 percent last year, and they've grown 60 percent," he said.

Nu-Kote recently bought Pelikan Products, its arch rival in ribbons and cartridges. Nu-Kote, which has had trouble digesting Pelikan, lost $40 million last year and has been sued by shareholders for mishandling the acquisition. Still, Ian Elliott, vice president for product management, said Nu-Kote would soon introduce new aftermarket products, including color toners for copiers.

The printer companies are fighting back as best they can. Hewlett-Packard has moved the refill holes on its ink-jet cartridges, rendering obsolete much of the refill equipment now in use. It has introduced a high-capacity toner cartridge that provides a 30 percent lower cost per page, and a five-cartridge package that sells for 15 percent less per cartridge. And it recently dropped prices on all its toner cartridges.

"The growing competition certainly heightened our sense of urgency," said Doug Johnson, general manager for laser jet supplies at Hewlett-Packard.

Lexmark, hoping to keep its cartridges out of the hands of refillers, now offers a "prebate" version—customers can pay $30 less for a toner cartridge if they agree to return the spent cartridge to Lexmark. Lexmark has contracted with a local nonprofit group to recondition the cartridges, and resells them itself.

"If a customer wants remanufactured cartridges, we're best off meeting the need ourselves," said William Duffy, Lexmark's vice president for worldwide supplies marketing.

The printer makers have also filed numerous lawsuits for patent and trademark infringement. Many aftermarket companies have countersued, charging the manufacturers with anticompetitive behavior.

Some suits the printer makers win—many aftermarket companies have been forced to make Hewlett-Packard's and Epson's logos less prominent on their packaging, and the courts have affirmed Hewlett-Packard's right to move the refill holes on its cartridges. Some they lose—the courts have upheld Repeat-O-Type Manufacturing Co.'s right to alter Hewlett-Packard cartridges, which it buys wholesale, and sell the now-refillable cartridges in a kit with extra ink. And some are still pending—Nu-Kote remains in court with Hewlett-Packard, Epson and Canon.

The manufacturers' new aggressiveness has taken its toll. "Other people are promoting refill products, while we're spending our time fighting Hewlett," said Fred Keen, Repeat-O-Type's director of sales, who says the company lost money in each of the last four years, on revenues that fell 50 percent, to $2 million.

And all the aftermarket companies are feeling the pricing pressure. "The intense competition is forcing all of our prices to go down," said Jeffrey Johnson, Nashua's product manager for laser toner cartridges.

Of course, the printer manufacturers could throttle the aftermarket by recycling their own cartridges. Hewlett tried once, but found the quality hard to keep up. But now Lexmark is trying it, and many aftermarket executives figure it is a matter of time before others jump in.

The Race Is On in Printer-Supply Aftermarket
Claudia H. Deutsch

"The name brand companies will realize that if you can't beat us, join us," said Russ Kalvin, JR Inkjet's marketing director. "I hope they don't. But they will."

The New York Times, April 20, 1998
http://www.nytimes.com/library/tech/98/04/biztech/articles/20printer.html

CRITICAL THINKING QUESTIONS

1. How do changing technologies and changing consumer trends influence aftermarkets?
2. Aside from printers, what are other areas/products with promising aftermarkets? Who are the major players in these aftermarkets and what are their marketing strategies?
3. How do you expect the Web to influence future competition for aftermarket supplies?

STORY-SPECIFIC QUESTIONS

1. Briefly explain three steps that Hewlett-Packard has taken to protect its ink-cartridge market.
2. How has the Web changed competition in the printer aftermarket supply business?

SHORT APPLICATION ASSIGNMENTS

1. In teams or individually, answer the story-specific questions; keep your answers to 25–75 words for each question.
2. In teams of three to five persons, or as a whole class, discuss your responses to the critical thinking questions.
3. Prepare a one-page memo report (200–50 words) to your instructor in which you summarize this article. You will find a model one-page report on the Web site (nytimes.swcollege.com).
4. Write an executive summary (200–250 words). As an administrative assistant to a busy executive, you are expected to summarize selected articles and present important points. You will find a model executive summary on the Web site.
5. Summarize this article (100–125 words) for your company's newsletter. You will find a model newsletter article on the Web site.
6. In teams or individually, shop for the same printer supplies from three of the Web sites mentioned in the story. Your instructor may assign you a specific item. You may also be asked to report your results in a five-minute presentation or in a one-page memo.

BUILDING RESEARCH SKILLS

1. Individually or in teams, review three of the Web sites mentioned in the story. Your instructor may ask you to submit a three- to five-page marketing strategy or post a Web page, along with a letter of transmittal explaining the project. Here is one area to consider: How are the sites similar and how do they differ in marketing their supplies?
2. Using at least three other references (e.g., books, research-journal articles, newspaper or magazine stories or credible Web sites), write an 800- to 1,000-word essay addressing two of the critical thinking questions offered earlier. Assume that this essay will be used as an internal reference for a corporation's marketing plan.
3. Using at least three other references (e.g., books, research-journal articles, newspaper or magazine stories or credible Web sites), post an 800- to 1,000-word Web page addressing at least two of the earlier critical thinking questions. Assume that this page will be posted in the marketing section of a corporate intranet.

Microsoft Is Busy on Several Legal Fronts

By Lawrence M. Fisher

Microsoft's legal department could keep a travel agent fully occupied these days. In addition to dispatching lawyers from Redmond, Wash., to federal court in Washington, D.C., the company is currently defending itself against lawsuits filed by software companies in San Jose, Calif., Salt Lake City and Bridgeport, Conn.

Although Microsoft has said these three other suits are without merit, it has so far been notably unsuccessful in its efforts to have them dismissed or delayed—or to have a change of venue to the presumably less burdensome and friendlier environs of Redmond. And the possibility exists that any evidence dug up in these corporate suits could reinforce the government's case.

Whatever the differences among the three competitor suits, all make the same contention that lies at the heart of the federal-state antitrust suit against Microsoft: They argue that the company has tried to use its dominance to forestall competition.

The oldest of these three pending suits was filed in July 1996 by Caldera Inc., of Orem, Utah, which sells DR-DOS, a competitor to Microsoft's MS-DOS, the operating system underlying Windows. The next, filed in October 1997, came from Sun Microsystems Inc., of Palo Alto, Calif., the creator of Java, a programming language. The most recent, filed in August, was brought by Bristol Technology Inc., of Danbury, Conn., which makes software tools that enable programs originally written to run on Windows to also run on other operating systems.

Like any large corporation, Microsoft over the years has been the subject of many legal actions. It has won some of these—notably in 1992, after years in court, when a judge ruled against Apple Computer Inc.'s claim that Microsoft's Windows software infringed on Macintosh copyrights. The software giant has lost some—like tiny Stac Electronics Inc.'s 1994 claim for patent infringement, which resulted in Microsoft's settling the matter by buying a majority interest in Stac.

And Microsoft has settled others, most recently, for undisclosed terms, a licensing dispute with AT&T over access to the programming code underlying Microsoft's Windows NT software.

But it is the pending the suits by Caldera, Sun and Bristol that are most noteworthy right now because of their parallels with the federal-state antitrust case.

Caldera filed its antitrust suit against Microsoft on July 24, 1996, the same day it completed the acquisition of the DR-DOS product from Novell Inc. (Novell had acquired the program's creator, Digital Research Inc., in 1991.) Although DR-DOS essentially duplicated the functions of MS-DOS, Microsoft could never challenge the product on legal grounds because MS-DOS itself was derived from CPM, an older operating system created by Digital Research.

Any chance for competition in desktop computing between MS-DOS and DR-DOS is now history. But Caldera officials see a market opportunity for DR-DOS in small hand-held devices, where their product competes with Microsoft's version of Windows for consumer-electronics products, called Windows CE. And Caldera's suit alleges that Microsoft used its market power to thwart sales of DR-DOS through unfair pricing practices and license agreements, as well as false statements and "vaporware" announcements suggesting that improved versions of MS-DOS were forthcoming.

"We felt as a smaller company we were in a unique position to bring the lawsuit forward," said Bryan Sparks, chief executive of Caldera, which is majority owned by Raymond J. Noorda, former head of Novell. "We weren't beholden to Microsoft for anything," Sparks said, "so if they were to retaliate, they couldn't do much."

One of the more striking claims to come from Caldera's suit is the testimony leaked to the news media that is said to have been given in the deposition of Stefanie Reichel, a former Microsoft account manager in Germany. According

---

LEGAL IMBROGLIOS
Even as Microsoft gears up to defend itself against a Government antitrust lawsuit, the company is also facing three lawsuits from competitors.

Competitor: Caldera
Accusation: Predatory practices
Caldera says that Microsoft used its market muscle and unfair pricing practices and licensing agreements to thwart sales of DR-DOS, a computer operating system that competes with Microsoft's MS-DOS.

Competitor: Sun Microsystems
Accusation: Breach of contract
Sun says that after it allowed Microsoft to license its Java programming language, Microsoft made unauthorized modifications so that the software would work only on computers running Microsoft's Windows operating system.

Competitor: Bristol Technology
Accusation: Predatory control of the Windows programming code
Bristol licensed the Microsoft code for creating Windows programs so that Bristol's software, Wind/U, could enable programs to run on Unix systems. Now that Microsoft has a competitor to Unix, Windows NT, Bristol says that Microsoft has made it impossible to update the license.

Microsoft Is Busy on Several Legal Fronts
Lawrence M. Fisher

to lawyers familiar with her testimony, Ms. Reichel's deposition alluded to the destruction and withholding of evidence that would have been relevant to the Justice Department's previous investigation of Microsoft, which the company settled in 1995.

At a hearing in Salt Lake City on Sept. 28, Microsoft requested that Caldera be served with a contempt order, claiming it was illegally sharing confidential information safeguarded by protective order. But U.S. District Judge Ronald Boyce granted Caldera the right to attempt to substantiate Ms. Reichel's testimony. The judge also denied Microsoft's request for a 120-day delay of the trial, which is scheduled to begin next June.

Microsoft contends that MS-DOS has been totally subsumed by the Windows 95 and Windows 98 operating systems and that any competitive issues with DR-DOS were covered in the 1995 Justice Department settlement. But Caldera officials assert that MS-DOS is alive and well and running under Windows 95 and 98—just as it did under earlier versions of Windows.

"We can run Windows 95 or 98 on top of DR-DOS; they are absolutely separable," Sparks said. "Windows 95 is essentially a walking antitrust violation because it ties together two products with no benefit to the consumer."

In the case of Sun Microsystems, which filed its suit on Oct. 7, 1997, the issue is breach of contract and false advertising, not antitrust. And yet, this suit, too, accuses Microsoft of anti-competitive behavior. Sun's suit, filed just two weeks before the Justice Department set in motion the legal events leading to the impending Government antitrust trial, stems from a license Sun granted to Microsoft in 1996 to use and distribute Java—a Sun technology and programming language for use on the Internet. One of the key features of Java is that programs written with it are supposed to work with any operating system.

But Microsoft made modifications to the Java code that allows its version of Java to work only with Windows computers. In Sun's view, this Windows tailoring negates the cross-platform purpose of Java and violates the terms of Microsoft's license. Last March in San Jose, Federal Judge Ronald Whyte made an interim ruling in Sun's favor, issuing a preliminary injunction that forbids Microsoft from using a Java-compatible logo on its products.

Sun is now seeking to block all Microsoft shipments of Java-based products that do not meet its compatibility tests. At a hearing in San Jose on Sept. 10, Sun's attorney, Lloyd (Rusty) Day, argued that Microsoft wanted "to kill cross-platform Java and grow the polluted Java market" by encouraging software developers to abandon its cross-platform ability.

Mr. Day focused his remarks on a Microsoft Java product called VJ++ 6.0, a new software "tool kit" for creating Java-based programs. VJ++ 6.0, he said, forces outside software developers to create Java programs that are "locked into the products that Microsoft alone distributes."

But Microsoft's lawyer, Karl Quackenbush, said the case was fundamentally about a contract, in which he said "Microsoft got broad rights to modify, adapt, create, derivative works of the technology."

Mr. Quackenbush said the features added to VJ++ 6.0 did not violate the licensing agreement because software developers were free to turn them off if they wished and to create Sun-standard Java programs with the product. "Maybe Sun wishes Microsoft would not have gone forward and made these enhancements," he said. "That doesn't mean it's a breach of contract."

The most recent suit alleging anti-competitive behavior against Microsoft came from Bristol, which filed on Aug. 18. The suit contends that Microsoft injured Bristol and the rest of the software industry through "predatory" control of the Windows application programming interfaces—the bits of codes that outside programmers use to assure that their products will work properly with the Windows operating system.

At issue is Bristol's product Wind/U, a program that lets Windows programs run on computers that use the Unix operating system. Bristol executives said they had initially developed Wind/U without access to Microsoft application programming code, but modified it after Microsoft granted Bristol a license in 1994. Although Microsoft then publicly endorsed Bristol's products for several years, Bristol said Microsoft was now refusing to update the license to cover Microsoft Windows NT 4.0, Windows NT 5.0 and subsequent releases—at least not under terms that Bristol says are technically or economically viable.

"I think that what happened was NT got this big share of the market, then Microsoft said now that we've got this foothold we no longer want people to run Windows applications on Unix," said Keith Blackwell, Bristol's president and chief executive.

Microsoft, however, says that Bristol's private antitrust suit, like the Government's case, is groundless. Jim Cullinan, a Microsoft spokesman, said Bristol had sought to license Windows NT 4.0 and 5.0 at the same terms as it paid for NT 3.0, even though the later programs are considerably larger.

"We thought negotiations were ongoing until Bristol filed this suit," Mr. Cullinan said, adding that Bristol's primary competitor, Mainsoft Inc., "has signed a contract accepting terms very similar to what we offered Bristol."

Bristol seeks an injunction, pending a trial, that would prevent Microsoft from blocking Bristol's access to Windows source code. A hearing in Bridgeport is scheduled for this Wednesday—less than a week before Microsoft's trial is to begin in Washington next Monday.

The New York Times, October 12, 1998
http://www.nytimes.com/library/tech/98/10/biztech/articles/12microsoft-lawsuits.html

CRITICAL THINKING QUESTIONS

1. Has Microsoft used its market dominance to thwart competition? Why, or why not?
2. Should anti-trust laws exist? Why, or why not? Should the free-market economy be allowed to prosper unfettered by government legislation? Why, or why not?
3. Why, if at all, should exceptions be made for companies competing in the fast-moving software industry?
4. How could Microsoft's lawsuits influence a software company's marketing environment?

STORY-SPECIFIC QUESTIONS

1. Briefly explain the three lawsuits filed against Microsoft.
2. What past experience has Microsoft had with similar lawsuits?

SHORT APPLICATION ASSIGNMENTS

1. In teams or individually, answer the story-specific questions; keep your answers to 25–75 words for each question.
2. In teams of three to five persons, or as a whole class, discuss your responses to the critical thinking questions.
3. Prepare a one-page memo report (200–250 words) to your instructor in which you summarize this article. You will find a model one-page report on the Web site (nytimes.swcollege.com).
4. Write an executive summary (200–250 words). As an administrative assistant to a busy executive, you are expected to summarize selected articles and present important points. You will find a model executive summary on the Web site.
5. Summarize this article (100–125 words) for your company's newsletter. You will find a model newsletter article on the Web site.
6. In teams or individually, search the New York Times on the Web for an update on the Microsoft lawsuits. Your instructor may assign you a specific lawsuit. You may also be asked to report your results in a five-minute presentation or one-page memo.

BUILDING RESEARCH SKILLS

1. Individually or in teams, draft a marketing policy for an organization; the policy should address the legal issues raised by the Microsoft lawsuits. Your instructor may give you a sample organization. You may also be asked to submit a three- to five-page policy handbook or post a Web page, along with a letter of transmittal explaining the project.
2. Individually or in teams, analyze an organization's anti-competitive practices. Your instructor may give you a sample organization. You may also be asked to submit a three- to five-page paper or post a Web page summarizing your findings.

Chapter 3
The Marketing Environment

3. Using at least three other references (e.g., books, research-journal articles, newspaper or magazine stories or credible Web sites), write an 800- to 1,000-word essay addressing two of the critical thinking questions offered earlier. Assume that your essay will be used as an internal reference for an organization's marketing plan.
4. Using at least three other references (e.g., books, research-journal articles, newspaper or magazine stories or credible Web sites), post an 800- to 1,000-word Web page addressing at least two of the earlier critical thinking questions. Assume that this page will be posted in the policy section of a corporate intranet.

CHAPTER 4

Marketing Research

PREVIEW

To make the right decisions, marketing managers need the right information about the right market variables at the right time—an ongoing data-stream from which to address an ever-changing marketplace.

The World Wide Web gives market researchers a new and wholly unique research tool, access to an online global library with "teraflops" of information. Unlike traditional libraries, Web pages are hard to catalog and track; there is no central control over this online library's "books."

Moreover, since Web pages change constantly and can easily be deleted, should they be trusted? Tina Kelley's "Whales in the Minnesota River?" provides amusing examples as well as basic guidelines for using the Web's vast storehouse of timely information.

In addition to misleading information, market researchers have an obligation to be aware of such issues as data security, user privacy, consumer protection, intellectual property, fair-use, trademarks and copyright. Attention to and appreciation of these concerns is not only proper, it also can be a legal obligation; thanks to technology, attention to these issues should increase. Bob Tedeschi updates an ongoing privacy concern in "Net Companies Look Offline for Consumer Data."

Source: Christine M. Thompson/CyberTimes

Whales in the Minnesota River?
Only on the Web, Where Skepticism Is a Required Navigational Aid

By Tina Kelley

Tourists drove six hours to Mankato, Minn., in search of underground caves and hot springs mentioned on a Web site. When they arrived, there were no such attractions.

People searching for a discussion of Amnesty International's views on Tunisia learned about human rights in that North African country—but from supporters of the Tunisian authorities, not from the human rights group. The government supporters brought surfers to a site with a soothing Web address: www.amnesty-tunisia.org.

And bibliophiles who trust the grande dame of on-line retailers, Amazon.com, for suggestions under the headings of "Destined for Greatness" and "What We're Reading" were dismayed to learn that some publishers had paid for special treatment for their books—meaning a more accurate heading would have been "What We're Paid to Say We're Reading." (After the disclosure, Amazon added a note on its home page to make a subtle acknowledgement of the practice.)

On the World Wide Web, straight facts can be hard to find. After plowing through dense and recalcitrant search engines that offer more sites than you can point a mouse at, after enduring delays, lost links and dead ends and arriving at a site that looks just right, Web surfers must deal with uncertainty: Is the information true, unbiased and free of hidden sales pitches?

Even though it is easy to fall prey to parodies, politics, payola and ignorance on line, solid, watertight information can indeed be found on the Web.

But experts on Internet research point out that the Web is largely unregulated and unchecked, and so they agree that it is wise to be skeptical: Consider the source. Reconsider the source. Is the information up to date and professional and traceable? Can it be verified, or the source checked, off line? And just who was that source again?

Don Ray, a freelance investigative reporter in Burbank, Calif., and the author of *Checking Out Lawyers* (MIE Publishing, 1997), has what he calls a J.D.L.R. test to apply to Web research. "There should be a switch in every Internet user that toggles when something Just Doesn't Look Right," he said, "to make them reevaluate the credibility of the source." If a Web page has grammatical errors, sloppy spelling or a goofy design, that makes him distrust the content.

And people who are getting ready to spend money on the basis of Web information should, of course, approach their decisions with at least as much skepticism as they would use about a purchase off line.

Whales in the Minnesota River?
Tina Kelley

Whoppers have found a home on the Web since the very beginning. Yet for many people, computers have generally been treated as authority figures, able to calculate compound interest in a single bound. A machine that has been perfected by institutions of higher learning and is relied on by the Government isn't likely to lie, is it?

"We've inherited this notion that if it pops up on a screen and looks good, we tend to think of it as fairly credible," said Paul Gilster, author of "Digital Literacy" (Wiley Computer Publishing, 1997.)

Although the Web has come to resemble a monstrous library system where everyone has a printing press and all information is seemingly created equal, even the newest surfers come to it with useful information-sorting skills from the off-line world. They can differentiate among information from a trusted newspaper, a bulk mailing from a charity, a sales pitch from a stockbroker and a letter from a friend. They can distinguish commercial broadcasts from public television programs. They can skim over the pages in *Reader's Digest* with "Advertisement" printed at the top.

But on the Web, the clues for credibility are different, and so are the tools needed to assess the information.

How can someone know if a favorite portal site is making a nanobuck in sales commission every time the person buys something at the florist featured on the page? Comments from people who are either touting or trashing a stock on the Web for their own financial gain have been investigated repeatedly by the Federal Government. And is that medical information on that site underwritten by a drug company or by someone on drugs?

Research specialists agree on the importance of determining who finances a site and what profit motives may be at work. While the boundary between news material and advertising is fairly clearly marked in many print publications, on the Web the signals pointing to paid content are often subtle or nonexistent, or vary widely from site to site.

Amazon.com's practice is only the most visible of many arrangements between Internet companies—including one involving *The New York Times*.

The Web site of *The Times* includes, on book review pages, links to Barnesandnoble.com; *The Times* receives commissions from the resulting sales.

Of course, off-line retail stores—including bookstores and groceries—have long accepted pay for product placement.

And being a knowledgeable consumer is important on line as well as off line.

At Time Warner's Pathfinder Network, Andrew Weil's theories on vitamins and health are used to create a profile of your vitamin needs and—surprise, surprise—sell you vitamins at the end (cgi.pathfinder .com/drweil/vitamin profiler).

Or consider www.smokefreekids.com, which presents all kinds of information on smoke-free dining and how to kick the nicotine habit—and won't let visitors miss out on the opportunity to buy No Smoke software to quit smoking.

Even outright spoofs can deceive the unwary Web traveler. Take the case of a site posted through Mankato State University by people fed up with the cold winters. The Mankato, Minn., Home Page advertised sunny beaches, an underwater city and whale watching on the Minnesota River (www.lme.mankato.msus.edu/mankato/mankato.html). Deep at the bottom of the disclaimer page one finds: "Mankato, as portrayed on these pages, DOES NOT EXIST! PLEASE do not come here to see these sites." Er, sights. (Of course, anybody looking at a map would probably be suspicious about the site's statement that "the winter temperature in many Mankato neighborhoods has never dropped below a balmy 70 degrees!")

That Mankato site "has caused some bad publicity for us," said Maureen Gustafson, head of the Mankato Area Chamber and Convention Bureau. "There was a guy who drove here from Canada with his son who was really ticked," she said. "And another one from Kansas."

She wrote the site's creator a letter—which he later posted, to her dismay—suggesting that he and his companions go play with Game Boys rather than undercut the city's promotional efforts.

Some Web sites appear designed to mislead or even intercept surfers, sometimes for political reasons. For instance, to counter what it calls intentionally misleading information, Amnesty International, the human rights group, has posted www.amnesty.org/tunisia, which includes point-by-point refutations of the site at www.amnesty-tunisia.org, which Amnesty calls "official Tunisian Internet propaganda." The Internet addresses of the pages are, of course, very close, adding to the confusion. But most surfers who wanted impartial information about Tunisia would perhaps choose not to rely on a site that prominently features a quotation from the president of Tunisia, Zine el-Abidine Ben Ali.

In a medium where truth is so elusive, medical misinformation is all too easy to find. Beth Mark, a librarian at Messiah College in Grantham, Pa., said a friend had sent her husband, Ken, an article from a commercial Web site (munkey.com/health/markle.html) about the health risks of the artificial sweetener aspartame. Mr. Mark, a diabetic, had recently suffered a mini-stroke, and he became worried after reading in the article that aspartame in the sodas he drinks could cause numbness, a claim that is generally not supported by scientific studies, although other questions have been raised about aspartame.

"It is sensational and contains unfounded claims regarding aspartame causing symptoms of M.S., numbness, etc.," Mrs. Mark said of the article, via e-mail.

Soon after, a senior medical adviser to the Multiple Sclerosis Foundation, Dr. David Squillacote, posted a refutation of the article's claims (www.msfacts.org/aspartame.htm).

Deborah Cestone, head of the library and media department at the Pelham Memorial High School and Middle School in Pelham, N.Y., teaches students how to evaluate Web sources for their research papers.

"You'll find sites like the University of Pennsylvania Cancer Center, and you know that's good solid information, but then you'll find a paper done by some 10th grader as a project, and he's created a Web page from it," she said.

After all, anyone with an Internet service provider and a quarter to call it can set up a Web page that looks as official as a 1040 form, without the quality control that used to come from editors, fact checkers and large publishing houses. There are few barriers to bad information on line.

"If you wanted to publish a book that says 2 plus 2 equals 5, you had to go through a lot of effort and spend a great deal of money," said Tara Calishain, co-author of *The Official Netscape Guide to Internet Research* (International Thomson Publishing, 1998). "But the cost of putting up a Web page saying 2 plus 2 equals 5 is virtually nothing."

Genie Tyburski, a law librarian in Philadelphia, runs a site about reliable research on line (www.virtualchase.com), which includes pointers on how to avoid being duped. "Many of us who are my age, 41, grew up trusting print," she said. "If we read it, it must have been true. We translate that same comfort to the Web, where it's much more dangerous."

She recalled a Web site about the medical uses of marijuana that had been run from a man's personal home page. It included copies of articles from medical journals but no mention of permission to reproduce them, she said.

"With the technology of the Web, there's no barrier to editing," she said. "An entire interview reproduced in the article on the bogus site was not in the original article at all, and there were graphs to support certain statements that weren't in the original article."

Rob Rosenberger, a computer security expert, set up a Web site to dispel myths about computer viruses (www.kumite.com).

"I just claim to be unaligned, but how do you know that?" Mr. Rosenberger said in an interview. To encourage critical thinking, he has a link on his site titled "Learn About Rob Before You Start Taking His Advice," which dares people to treat his writing with the same skepticism he brings to virus scares.

Of course, it is hard to know who is paying whom for what kind of Internet presence. "There are the ones we know about, like Amazon.com, which got caught," Mr. Rosenberger said.

"But there are unscrupulous people in the securities industry who are trying to pump up or drive down stocks, to buy at low prices and sell at high prices, who may not be disclosing their fiduciary interests."

"People send out spams on the greatest I.P.O. on the Internet this year, or trash an I.P.O. that's going to occur, so they can get in at the low end," Mr. Rosenberger said. "We know that goes on, too."

Mr. Gilster, the author of *Digital Literacy*, said Internet users need to be trained to triangulate in on the truth.

"We need to set up content evaluation as part of the intellectual superstructure here and explain it to kids," he said, "so we end up with students who can use the Web intelligently and know when to cast grave doubt on a particular Web site. People have to be their own editors and take that upon themselves. Once you begin doing that, the habits become second nature."

But some questions about the validity of Web sources are impossible to answer beyond a reasonable doubt without stepping outside the hermetic box of the Internet. In such cases, no combination of pixels is sure to help.

"When you want to check citations, your librarian is your best friend," Ms. Calishain said. "There's a lot of stuff on line, but working with librarians is one of best things you can do with research. They're trained to classify information, and they can help you out."

It is also true that many librarians are learning to navigate the world of the Web, and they may just point an information-hungry consumer elsewhere.

Ms. Cestone, the Pelham school librarian, said she worked hard teaching students how to evaluate what might be the best resource for a given research problem.

"It may be the Internet is the best resource, or maybe a book, or maybe a person will be the best resource," she said.

The New York Times, March 4, 1999
http://www.nytimes.com/library/tech/99/03/circuits/articles/04trut.html

CRITICAL THINKING QUESTIONS

1. Should the information that any Web site provides automatically be considered true, unbiased and free of hidden sales pitches? Why, or why not?
2. How and why would organizations or individuals post Web sites that contain false or misleading information?
3. What, if anything, can be done to keep false or misleading information from the Web?
4. Ideally, what guidelines should consumers use to evaluate information found on the Web?

STORY-SPECIFIC QUESTIONS

1. Briefly explain three examples of false or misleading information found on the Web.
2. Briefly explain three possible guidelines for evaluating information found on the Web.

SHORT APPLICATION ASSIGNMENTS

1. In teams or individually, answer the story-specific questions; keep your answers to 25–75 words for each question.
2. In teams of three to five persons, or as a whole class, discuss your responses to the critical thinking questions.

3. Write an executive summary (200–250 words). As an administrative assistant to a busy executive, you are expected to summarize selected articles and present important points. You will find a model executive summary on the Web site (nytimes.swcollege.com).
4. Search the Web for information on a topic of your choice. Next, evaluate the credibility of the first three Web sites returned by the search engine you used. Which of those three sites would you trust and why? Your instructor may ask you to share your results in a five-minute presentation or one-page memo.

BUILDING RESEARCH SKILLS

1. Using at least three other references (e.g., books, research-journal articles, newspaper or magazine stories or credible Web sites), write an 800- to 1,000-word essay addressing two of the critical thinking questions offered earlier. Assume that your essay will be a background document for a corporation's research guidelines.
2. Using at least three other references (e.g., books, research-journal articles, newspaper or magazine stories or credible Web sites), post an 800- to 1,000-word Web page addressing at least two of the earlier critical thinking questions. Assume that your page will be a background document for a corporation's research guidelines.

Net Companies Look Offline for Consumer Data

By Bob Tedeschi

Last week's announcement that the Internet advertising firm DoubleClick Inc. planned to merge with Abacus Direct Corp., a company that sells information about consumers' catalogue purchases, raised more than the two companies' stock prices.

It also raised the hackles of privacy advocates, who said the merger would yield intrusive or abusive Internet marketing practices, and pledged to file a complaint with the Federal Trade Commission to block the deal. But the privacy groups may be a bit late to the game.

The reality is that Internet advertising companies are already far along in their effort to marry offline and online customer information.

The practice of using data gathered offline to bolster online marketing "is growing by leaps and bounds," said Jim Nail, online advertising analyst with Forrester Research, an Internet research firm. "Advertisers are beginning to understand the potential power of that data online."

The DoubleClick/Abacus deal, which is set to close in September, will merge the two companies under the DoubleClick name. The fruits of this partnership, company officials hope, will include the ability to serve Internet "banner" ads to users based on what they have purchased offline in the past.

Until now, Internet advertisers have typically had to settle for analyzing the demographic data collected about visitors to a particular site and make educated guesses about their purchasing behavior. In the future, that decision will increasingly be informed by information about an individual's offline purchasing history.

If a consumer has bought, for instance, golfing equipment from a print catalogue, DoubleClick will be able to recognize that customer when he arrives at one of the 7,400 sites that either use DoubleClick's ad server technology or belong to the DoubleClick network. At that point, the company can instantaneously review the consumer's spending habits and serve an ad for other golfing items.

The technology depends on the use of "cookies," data files that sites embed on a user's browser, which can be used to track visitors as they move through the site. Those cookies assign numbers to users, so they remain anonymous—until they give their name to a site during a transaction or registration. Once a site matches a number with a name, they know who is browsing, and can then look to one of the countless offline data companies to get more information about that individual.

DoubleClick is actually playing catch-up in this regard. One of DoubleClick's

Net Companies Look Offline for Consumer Data
Bob Tedeschi

chief rivals in the Internet advertising arena, 24/7 Media, is already matching cookie numbers with consumer names—and they're doing it in an unexpected way: when customers register new computer products for warranties online.

The company has an agreement with Intelliquest, a marketing firm that processes product registrations for roughly 85 percent of companies in this category who choose to outsource the task. That number translates to "well over a million [individuals] per month," according to C. Andrew Johns, 24/7's chief financial officer.

When a customer registers a product over the Internet with a company that works with Intelliquest—and during that process, agrees to accept future marketing messages—a cookie is assigned to that user's browser. Intelliquest then provides 24/7 with the cookie number and the person's name and address.

While the Intelliquest agreement represents 24/7's best source of cookie identification at the moment, Johns said the company is achieving the same goal with other methods as well, and will offer ads based on the data in the fourth quarter of this year.

If privacy groups were vexed by this new approach to advertising, perhaps it's because they know how much information is available offline. For example, Acxiom Corp., one of the biggest suppliers of customer information to marketing firms, has detailed data on 95 percent of the households in the United States. That includes an individual's name, address, occupation, and home value—and frequently, information on that person's hobbies, income, investments, and car. According to Don Hinman, who leads Acxiom's data content group, the company is "now getting more and more business from Internet marketers, but it's still early in the life cycle."

Executives and analysts agree that such information is crucial to the continued success of online advertising, which has struggled to live up to the hype—often generated by Internet companies themselves—that the Internet could provide a degree of marketing accuracy unattainable in other media.

As that promise has gone stale, advertisers have seen two critical measures of Internet advertising fall precipitously—so-called "click-through rates" and "CPMs." Click-through rates, the rate at which consumers actually click on advertising banners, have fallen to 0.5 percent from a rate of between 2 and 3 percent in 1996, executives said. CPMs, the cost to advertisers for each 1,000 ad banners displayed, have also fallen to between $10 and $15 this year, down from roughly $20 a year ago.

If better customer information leads to higher click-through rates, Web publishers should be able to command higher CPMs—and Internet advertising firms should also be able to command higher fees. "That's the theory anyway," said Johns, of 24/7. "Hopefully that's how it'll work."

Assuming that advertising firms can refine the technology to the point where they can sift through their databases and serve targeted ads instantaneously, the only thing that stands in the way of this next wave of advertising is the issue of consumer privacy. Privacy advocates have pledged to file a complaint with the FTC protesting the DoubleClick-Abacus merger, on the grounds that the new company would violate the standards of fair information collection by using data in ways not envisioned by consumers when they relinquished that information.

Industry executives, meanwhile, say the deal is not only perfectly legal, but may ultimately be welcomed by consumers. "The fact that DoubleClick will be able to offer ads that people will be more interested in will be positive both for consumers and for the Internet in general," said H. Robert Wientzen, president and chief executive of The Direct Marketing Association. "We need to work harder to make the Internet more profitable."

Kevin Ryan, president and chief operating officer of DoubleClick, agreed, and added that "we're one of the only players to offer consumers the chance to opt out of a cookie, and Abacus also offers people the ability to opt out" of catalogue marketing offers, he said. "If customers get full disclosure—and they will—and the ability to opt out, they're covered."

Still, Nail, of Forrester, said customers might not see the issues so clearly. "Privacy is potentially a huge sleeper issue," he said. "You see a lot of talk and some government action on it, but it hasn't really caught fire with the public yet. This has the potential to touch it off."

CyberTimes, The New York Times on the Web, June 21, 1999
http://www.nytimes.com/library/tech/99/06/cyber/commerce/21commerce.html

CRITICAL THINKING QUESTIONS

1. What restriction, if any, should be placed on the use of data gathered offline to bolster online marketing?
2. What are some of the probable scenarios whereby online marketers could benefit from using data gathered offline?
3. Who gathers offline consumer data, and what types of data do they gather?
4. What are the arguments for and against gathering consumer data?
5. What are the arguments for and against matching online- and offline-gathered consumer data?

STORY-SPECIFIC QUESTIONS

1. How do Internet advertisers typically gather data about Web-site visitors?
2. What are "cookies" and how can they be used in online advertising?

Net Companies Look Offline for Consumer Data
Bob Tedeschi

SHORT APPLICATION ASSIGNMENTS

1. In teams or individually, answer the story-specific questions; keep your answers to 25–75 words for each question.
2. In teams of three to five persons, or as a whole class, discuss your responses to the critical thinking questions.
3. Prepare a one-page memo report (200–250 words) to your instructor in which you summarize this article. You will find a model one-page report on the Web site (nytimes.swcollege.com).
4. Write an executive summary (200–250 words). As an administrative assistant to a busy executive, you are expected to summarize selected articles and present important points. You will find a model executive summary on the Web site.
5. Summarize this article (100–125 words) for your company's newsletter. You will find a model newsletter article on the Web site.
6. In teams or individually, review the *New York Times on the Web*'s privacy information. With what parts of it do you agree, and why? To what parts of it do you object, and why? Your instructor may ask you to share your results in a five-minute presentation or one-page memo.
7. In teams or individually, review a Web site's privacy policy. With what parts of it do you agree, and why? To what parts of it do you object, and why? Your instructor may assign you a specific Web site. You may also be asked to share your results in a five-minute presentation or one-page memo.

BUILDING RESEARCH SKILLS

1. Individually or in teams, review the privacy policies of three Web sites. How are they similar? How do they differ? You may choose from among the sites listed on the New York Times on the Web's privacy information page, or your instructor may assign you Web sites. Your instructor may also ask you to submit a three- to five-page policy handbook or post a Web page, along with a letter of transmittal explaining the project.
2. Individually or in teams, analyze your school's privacy policy. With what parts of it do you agree, and why? To what parts of it do you object, and why? Your instructor may ask you to submit a three- to five-page paper or post a Web page summarizing your findings, along with a letter of transmittal explaining the project.
3. Using at least three other references (e.g., books, research-journal articles, newspaper or magazine stories or credible Web sites), write an 800- to 1,000-word essay addressing at least two of the earlier critical thinking questions. Assume that your essay will be used as an internal reference for a corporation's marketing plan.
4. Using at least three other references (e.g., books, research-journal articles, newspaper or magazine stories or credible Web sites), post an 800- to 1,000-word Web page addressing at least two of the earlier critical thinking questions. Assume that your page will be posted in the policy section of a corporate intranet.

CHAPTER 5

Consumer Behavior

PREVIEW

Who buys what, when and where, for how much, and for what reason—that is the essential paradigm of the consumer behavior researcher. Myriad forces, both psychological and sociological, influence a consumer's product and service consumption patterns. Tracking trends in the marketplace and formulating the appropriate marketing mix based on these trends is the "raison d'être" for the marketing manager.

Identifying and responding to a marketing trend can be profitable if it is responded to quickly and correctly. As Bob Tedeschi observes in "Online Retailers Applaud Increase in Women Shoppers," e-commerce merchants are trying to profit from a recent trend—an increase in the number of women using the Internet for shopping.

Consumer research also involves the study of physiological influences on consumer decision-making processes. Businesses, for example, are paying attention to environmental fragrancing. Herein, the old adage that consumers can always smell a good deal is truly put to the test in Kate Murphy's "A Sales Pitch Right Under Your Nose."

Source: Christine M. Thompson/CyberTimes

Online Retailers Applaud Increase in Women Shoppers

By Bob Tedeschi

While the e-commerce engine has been warming up in recent months, it remains fueled largely by the wallets of affluent men and computer geeks. That fuel, however, is about to receive a powerful additive: X chromosomes.

Women are joining the Internet more quickly than ever, nearly erasing the gap among the medium's 92 million users. Perhaps more significant for the Internet economy, though, is the fact that the percentage of World Wide Web shoppers who are women has jumped the last 12 months, to 38 percent from 29 percent, according to a Commercenet/Nielsen Media Research study. Industry executives expect that presence to rise quickly in the next year, bringing with it new opportunities in several categories and expanding e-commerce as a whole.

"The early part of the e-commerce revolution was a revolution of rich white males," said Katherine Borsecnik, senior vice president for strategic business at America Online. "That's changing. And with 80 to 85 percent of household spending controlled by women, the total retail dollars involved in that change is very high."

Of course, the immediate impact of that change will be felt in traditional female retail strongholds, said Fiona Swerdlow, an analyst with Jupiter Communications, the Internet research firm. Ms. Swerdlow forecasts that categories like apparel, health and beauty and toys will particularly benefit from a growing presence of women shoppers—meaning sites like those for Gap, Lands' End, Estee Lauder's Clinique, eToys and Toys "R" Us should benefit.

Not only will these categories benefit from first-time buyers, executives said, but they will also reap the fruits of higher spending from more experienced female Internet shoppers. Indeed, according to a survey by NFO Interactive conducted last week, women who shopped on the Internet in the last year said they planned to spend 20 percent more online in the next year. The survey gathered responses from 880 U.S. Internet users—437 of whom were women—who said they had bought goods over the Web in the last 12 months.

Travel and apparel are the most favored purchasing categories for female Internet shoppers, according to the survey. Women shoppers responding to the survey said they planned to spend, on average, $965 on travel and $783 on apparel online, respectively, on those categories in the next year.

The other online categories with the greatest growth potential among repeat buyers, according to NFO, include sports and fitness—on which the women in the survey said they planned to spend an average of 71 percent more this year than last. Others were food and drink (a projected spending increase of 27 percent), apparel and accessories (24 percent) and home and garden (13 percent).

"I've always said the Internet would take off when women came online, and it's true," said Marleen McDaniel, chief executive of Women.com, which offers information, shopping and advertising directed toward women. Women.com has catered to what Ms. McDaniel called characteristic shopping behavior among women—in particular, a propensity to gather a great deal of information before making a purchase. "Women are avid consumers of information, and shopping is their passion," Ms. McDaniel said.

Given that assumption, the site provides "tons of original content," she said, which women can use to make buying decisions. "We'll have an article on echinacea, within the subject of healing herbs," Ms. McDaniel said. "So we'll have a link next to it for colds, and what about echinacea makes it a remedy. Adjacent to that, we'll have an ad for a pharmacy that sells it. Then users can go to the community section of our site and ask a nutritionist, a woman doctor, when to take it. For advertisers, it's fantastic because you're catching a consumer right in flight."

The payoff is apparent in the site's shopping figures, Ms. McDaniel said. According to @Plan, an Internet research firm, 51 percent of Women.com's audience had made purchases on the Internet in the last six months, more than 10 percentage points higher than the average for women online.

Retailers are also using gender-specific approaches to cash in on perceived differences in shopping behavior. "We do a lot of things to skew toward women," said Steve Hamlin, vice president of iQVC, which is the online arm of Comcast Corp.'s QVC home-shopping TV channel and whose clientele is 70 percent female. "Women enjoy the experience of shopping more than men, and are more willing to look at content and browse the site."

For that reason, he said, areas of the site like the jewelry section and the wedding boutique include more editorial content and advisory features than, for instance, the area devoted to sporting goods.

Hamlin also said that the site had seen a significant rise in computer electronics purchases by women since it began selling prebundled systems. "Women generally feel less confident when making these kinds of purchases," he said, "so they're more comfortable knowing that a certain scanner goes with a certain computer."

Other sites take a more gender-neutral approach. Fingerhut, the Federated Department Stores subsidiary that wholly or partly owns several Web sites, including Andy's Garage and Mountainzone.com, "doesn't spend a lot of time looking at gender," said Andy Johnson, senior vice president for market development, even though 65 percent of Fingerhut's Internet shoppers are women. "We're trying to create processes to serve individual customers as much as they want, no matter their gender."

Online Retailers Applaud Increase in Women Shoppers
Bob Tedeschi

Ms. Borsecnik, of America Online, takes a similar view. "A vast majority of what we do has nothing to do with gender," she said, noting that roughly 50 percent of the company's shoppers are women. "Our approach is more of a translation of what works offline to the online world."

Because some retail categories that tend to attract women have not yet developed fully online, the gender impact may not be felt immediately, Ms. Borsecnik noted.

"Categories like house and garden hardly register among online shoppers, but offline, 25 to 30 percent of all purchases fall into that," she said. By contrast, Ms. Borsecnik said, music CDs account for 13 percent of all purchases made on America Online, while "music has to be less than 2 percent of offline purchases."

The growth in women shoppers may speed the maturation process for categories like house and garden, as companies rush to market—once they know the dollars are there. At the same time, Ms. Borsecnik said, many merchants are already setting up shop in hopes that doing so will give a greater number of women reason to log on, ready to spend. "There's still an element," she said, "of 'build it and they will come.'"

CyberTimes, The New York Times on the Web, July 12, 1999
http://www.nytimes.com/library/tech/99/07/cyber/commerce/12commerce.html

CRITICAL THINKING QUESTIONS

1. How could the growth and financial viability of e-commerce be influenced by an increase in the number of women going online?
2. Which commerce areas could dominate women's interests on the Internet? Why?
3. How do women and men differ in their offline shopping habits? How could this difference, or the uniqueness of women's offline shopping habits, shape the online shopping habits of women?
4. How, if at all, should Web sites ideally be designed for female shoppers? Why?

STORY-SPECIFIC QUESTIONS

1. What has been the growth in the occurrence of women shopping online?
2. Why do some Web sites have a "gender neutral" design?

SHORT APPLICATION ASSIGNMENTS

1. In teams or individually, answer the story-specific questions; keep your answers to 25–75 words for each question.
2. In teams of three to five persons, or as a whole class, discuss your responses to the critical thinking questions.

3. Prepare a one-page memo report (200–250 words) to your instructor in which you summarize this article. You will find a model one-page report on the Web site (nytimes.swcollege.com).
4. Write an executive summary (200–250 words). As an administrative assistant to a busy executive, you are expected to summarize selected articles and present important points. You will find a model executive summary on the Web site.
5. Summarize this article (100–125 words) for your company's newsletter. You will find a model newsletter article on the Web site.
6. In teams or individually, review one of the Web sites mentioned in the story as being designed specifically for women. Your instructor may ask you to share your results in a five-minute presentation or one-page memo. Here is one thing to consider in your review: How does the Web site's design cater to women?

BUILDING RESEARCH SKILLS

1. Individually or in teams, review three Web sites designed for women. You may choose from the sites mentioned in the story, or your instructor may assign you Web sites. How are they similar? How do they differ? You may also be asked to submit a three- to five-page policy handbook or post a Web page, along with a letter of transmittal explaining the project.
2. Individually or in teams, prepare a mock-up Web site that is designed for women. Your instructor may assign you a specific company or product for which to design the site. You may also be asked to submit a three- to five-page paper or post a Web page summarizing your findings.
3. Using at least three other references (e.g., books, research-journal articles, newspaper or magazine stories or credible Web sites), write an 800- to 1,000-word essay addressing two of the critical thinking questions offered earlier. Assume that this essay will be used as an internal reference for a corporation's marketing plan.
4. Using at least three other references (e.g., books, research-journal articles, newspaper or magazine stories or credible Web sites), post an 800- to 1,000-word Web page addressing at least two of the earlier critical thinking questions. Assume that this page will be posted in the policy section of a corporate intranet.

A Sales Pitch Right Under Your Nose

By Kate Murphy

Shoppers at the four Jordan's Furniture stores in Massachusetts and New Hampshire might be excused if they sense a hint of bubble gum in the children's room displays, or a whisper of pine in the country-style section.

It's not their imagination. Those fragrances are indeed wafting through those areas, part of an attempt by Jordan's to enlist the olfactory into making a sale.

"We want to appeal to all five senses in our displays," said Jan Hedrick, design director at Jordan's, which is based in Acton, Mass. "It makes the environment more interesting and makes people linger longer in the room, which makes them more likely to make a purchase."

Ms. Hedrick said sales have increased substantially since the chain incorporated scent into its retail marketing five years ago. And while she acknowledged that "it's impossible to pinpoint exactly how much of that is due to fragrance," Jordan's sells $900 of merchandise a square foot, compared with an industry average of $150 a year.

Coincidence? Perhaps. Buying decisions are based on many factors, and a scent is, by definition, an intangible.

But businesses are increasingly regarding "environmental fragrancing" as a key design element, as important as lighting, layout and background music. And traditional retailers in particular are looking for ways to make the store experience different from that of mail-order houses and Internet merchants.

The Christmas store at Disney World, which is open year-round, is infused with the scents of evergreen and spiced apple cider.

"It's difficult to conjure Christmas and the desire to do Christmas shopping in Florida in July," said David Martin, vice president of manufacturing at Fragrance Technologies, a company in Orlando, Fla., that outfitted the store.

With the help of those scents, he said, the store "smells like Christmas. It really gets you in the mood."

The Rainforest Cafe chain of 17 restaurants pumps fresh-flower extracts into its retail sections. "The scent opens your mind," said Steven W. Schussler, senior vice president of development at the company, which is based in Minneapolis. "It makes you curious and makes you more likely to spend money. Call it a subliminal awakening."

Fragrances may be one of the oldest marketing techniques—since ancient times, merchants have burned incense to draw a crowd. Walk past street vendors in Times Square and smell how the tradition continues today.

But for more subtle, nuanced approaches, only in the last 10 years has research focused on the effect of fragrances on moods and behavior. Studies in neurological, psychiatric and business management journals have shown that, like soft lighting and soothing music, pleasant smells can indeed have an influence.

"Interest has been ramping up with the popularity of aromatherapy," said Avery N. Gilbert, the scientific affairs director of the Olfactory Research Fund in New York, a division of the Fragrance Foundation, the industry's trade association. Aromatherapy, a type of alternative medicine, prescribes smelling herbs and essential oils to remedy various mental and physical disorders.

Moreover, new technologies analyze scents on a molecular level easily and cheaply, letting a growing industry of fragrance makers reproduce and sell them to businesses.

The effect of odors is thought to be more intense than auditory or visual stimuli because olfactory nerves connect directly to the area of the brain that is responsible for feelings and memory.

Research subjects who catch an appealing whiff of something like flowers, vanilla or cinnamon have tended to be more cooperative in negotiations and perform better on cognitive tasks—one reason that more corporations are installing fragrance systems at their work sites in an effort to improve productivity.

But retailers have focused on research showing that people evaluate merchandise more positively—and spend more time shopping—when an agreeable odor is present.

"Pleasant fragrances put you in a better mood," said Robert A. Baron, a professor of management and psychology at Rensselaer Polytechnic Institute in Troy, N.Y., who studies workplace and retail environments.

In one study, a fruity-floral scent introduced into a jewelry store was shown to increase lingering time. In another, people exposed to pleasant smells—coffee roasting, cookies baking—in one area of a shopping mall reported being in a better mood than those in fragrance-free areas.

They were also more likely to give a stranger change for a dollar and return dropped pens. The inference is that good smells make shoppers happier, more cooperative and, thus, more likely to buy.

Though the average person finds thousands of scents agreeable, selecting just the right one can be tricky. Not surprisingly, research shows that incongruent scents tend to decrease shoppers' interest.

That's probably why Victoria's Secret does not smell like pot roast—its stores are infused with the feminine scents the chain sells. "Fragrances should be an extension of corporate image," Gilbert said.

Indeed, Thomas Pink Inc., a London-based shirt maker that recently opened a store in Manhattan, fills its shops with the smell of "line-dried linen," said Robert F. Wood, director of the company's United States operations. "It's a very clean and crisp scent," he said, evoking "our product and its quality."

The New York Times, September 13, 1998
http://www.nytimes.com/library/financial/sunday/091398spend-smell.html

A Sales Pitch Right Under Your Nose
Kate Murphy

CRITICAL THINKING QUESTIONS

1. How could each of the five human senses influence a consumer's purchasing behavior?
2. How, if at all, could one of the five senses persuade a consumer to buy something that person does not want or need?
3. What new marketing applications could be developed for "environmental fragrancing" or aromatherapy?
4. From a marketing perspective, the use of scents for in-store environments can affect sales and influence consumer behavior. What promotional factors and olfactory scents would you use in a busy food court as opposed to using in an up-market women's clothing store?

STORY-SPECIFIC QUESTIONS

1. Briefly explain three examples of how fragrances have been used to influence consumer behavior.
2. According to what scientists now believe, how do fragrances affect consumer behavior?

SHORT APPLICATION ASSIGNMENTS

1. In teams or individually, answer the story-specific questions; keep your answers to 25–75 words for each question.
2. In teams of three to five persons, or as a whole class, discuss your responses to the critical thinking questions.
3. Prepare a one-page memo report (200–250 words) to your instructor in which you summarize this article. You will find a model one-page report on the Web site (nytimes.swcollege.com).
4. Write an executive summary (200–250 words). As an administrative assistant to a busy executive, you are expected to summarize selected articles and present important points. You will find a model executive summary on the Web site.
5. Summarize this article (100–125 words) for your company's newsletter. You will find a model newsletter article on the Web site.
6. In teams or individually, visit a local mall or shopping center. Did you encounter any intentional or unintentional "environmental fragrancing"? Your instructor may ask you to share your results in a five-minute presentation or one-page memo.

BUILDING RESEARCH SKILLS

1. Imagine you are the manager of a CD store that is near a coffee shop. You want to increase sales and need to apply olfactory senses as well as the other senses in a new marketing campaign. Your instructor may ask you to submit a three- to five-page marketing plan or post a Web page, along with a letter of transmittal explaining the campaign.

Chapter 5
Consumer Behavior

2. Using at least three other references (e.g., books, research-journal articles, newspaper or magazine stories or credible Web sites), write an 800- to 1,000- word essay addressing two of the critical thinking questions offered earlier. Assume that your essay will be used as an internal reference for a corporation's marketing plan.
3. Using at least three other references (e.g., books, research-journal articles, newspaper or magazine stories or credible Web sites), post an 800- to 1,000- word Web page addressing at least two of the earlier critical thinking questions. Assume that this page will be posted in the policy section of a corporate intranet.

CHAPTER 6

Market Segmentation

PREVIEW

"Different strokes for different folks" is the underlying logic of market segmentation. The fact is that different types of people (defined by demographic, psychographic, product use or behavioral variables) prefer different types of goods and services (defined by attributes such as quantity, price and style).

The key criteria for effective segmentation are that the segment can be accurately measured and located; the segment is meaningful in size and profitability; and the segment differentially responds to elements in the marketing mix.

Case in point: in "As Band of TV Channels Grows, Niche Programs Will Boom," Lawrie Mifflin documents the increasing number of new cable TV channels aimed at specific market segments. Marketers may target distinct market segments that can be defined and delineated solely by consumers' preferences for specific TV channels.

Similarly, Bob Tedeschi's "E-Commerce Sites Target Next Generation of Buyers" reports on the renewed discriminating power of the demographic variable of age. His article defines the nature and profitability of a target market segment—the "youth" market.

Source: Christine M. Thompson/CyberTimes

As Band of TV Channels Grows, Niche Programs Will Boom

By Lawrie Mifflin

For an aviation buff, the Discovery Wings cable channel is a dream come true—programs about planes and flying all day long.

Replace the aviation aficionado with a health nut hungry for the latest medical news (tuned to Discovery Health), or a do-it-yourselfer immersed in home renovations (Discovery Home and Leisure), or a schoolchild exploring ancient worlds (Discovery Civilization)—Discovery has a channel for each.

Meanwhile, MTV Networks, parent of MTV and VH1, has sprouted seven more offspring for different genres—VH1 Country, VH1 Soul, VH1 Smooth (jazz and "New Age" music), M2 (regular MTV on a different time schedule), MTV Ritmo (Latin music), MTV Rocks (hard rock and heavy metal) and MTV Indie (independent music and rap)—making a miniature radio dial on the television set.

Fewer than 2 million homes can receive these niche-within-a-niche cable channels, but they offer a glimpse of a vastly different media universe of the not-too-distant future, a world where an American audience already fragmented by myriad cable channels will be splintered into even tinier shards, as when Fox Family Channel recently announced the creation of separate networks for boys and girls.

Digital technology—which enables the television signal to be compressed to carry far more information—is ushering in this new age, when perhaps 1,400 or 1,500 choices will be on parade. Some of those choices will take forms people now associate with the computer rather than the television set, like bringing data to the screen, or Internet access, or interactive shopping, banking or video games.

The first tentative steps into this future are taking place, recalling the days when television itself was being created by people who, at first, tried simply to re-create popular radio shows on film. Television industry leaders today are as uncertain as they were then about how to use this new medium, and about what viewers will want from it.

"The transition to DTV is the biggest change in television history since television began," said Sandra Kresch, a partner in the entertainment and media division of PricewaterhouseCoopers, the giant business consulting firm. "Everyone has a vague idea of what the technology will produce; everyone has a vague idea of what consumers will want. But this has the potential to be so different from anything that's come before that nobody is really sure how it's going to develop."

Right now, digital cable television is transmitted primarily to cable systems around the country owned by Tele-Communications Inc.; since it was first

As Band of TV Channels Grows, Niche Programs Will Boom
Lawrie Mifflin

offered in late 1997, about 1.4 million cable customers have signed up for it. They get a package of 36 extra channels for $10 a month, and pay between $3 and $4 a month to rent a set-top box required to bring in the digital signal.

Digital signals can also provide high-definition television, or HDTV—pictures so crystalline and detailed that they look like Hieronymous Bosch paintings come to life. Most experts predict that HDTV sets' prices will stay high, moving from $7,000-plus now to around $3,000 in three years, and causing HDTV to take a decade or more to catch on.

But standard-definition digital television sets—with clearer pictures than current sets, and the capacity to pull in hundreds of channels—are a better bet for mass consumption. Experts say their prices will come down under the $1,000 mark within about three years' time.

For the near future, the average viewer with a digital television set will begin to see three main uses of the greater channel capacity: programs shown in high-definition format; many more channel choices (multicasting), or varied choices of starting times for movies and events (multiplexing).

"The consumer is being offered a decision," said Thomas Rogers, president of NBC Cable and executive vice president of NBC, a unit of General Electric Co. "Do they want more choices or prettier pictures? My guess is the answer will be a resounding vote for both."

But because the prettier pictures cost more to produce, and fewer people are likely to buy those expensive HDTV-ready sets, most experts think the industry will concentrate on greater choices—in programming and in data broadcasting. Viewing habits are expected to involve even narrower, more individually tailored and, eventually, interactive choices as digital television takes hold.

Take the example of the home fixer-upper who watches the Discovery Home and Leisure channel now. A rival, called the Do-It-Yourself Channel, is to start next year, as a spinoff of the Home and Garden Television network. And HGTV is developing another digital channel, called HGTV Professional, for builders, contractors, plumbers, landscapers and the like.

Critics worry that this will add more schlock and confusion to the television landscape, and that public-affairs programs and entrepreneurs with new program ideas will both be frozen out.

This issue is a question of capacity, and of who puts claims on that capacity. Each current broadcast station (like Channel 2 or 4 in New York) and each cable network "owns" the subdivisions of itself that digitalization will create. They will want to hold onto that real estate, so to speak, for the day when they find profitable ways to use it. The same is true for cable networks.

Federal law requires cable systems to carry the signals of local broadcast stations (in addition to whatever cable networks they carry). Station owners want that requirement extended, so that cable has to carry all the subchannels of Channel 2, for example, not just the main analog Channel 2. But cable operators argue that if they must carry all those channels, nonprofit networks like C-Span and community public access channels could get squeezed out—unless government regulations were passed to protect them.

Public television, too, awaits action from either Congress or the Federal Communications Commission on whether cable systems must carry all its channel offerings. And while public television programmers have many ideas for new educational or public-service uses of the added channels, they need to find ways to finance them.

Meanwhile, programmers are trying to position themselves in the new universe.

That is why A&E Networks (which is jointly owned by Walt Disney Co., Hearst Corp. and NBC) has started the Biography Channel and the International History Channel, expanding on two of its most popular existing program brands.

"It's like rolling the dice right now," said Nikolas Davatzes, A&E Networks' president. "I said to myself, 'I'm not sure where this ship is going, but I'm getting on it.' I don't want to be in a position of finding out they discovered America and I'm not there because I'm still in Greece tending my sheep."

But in the rush to gain a foothold on cable systems, some cable networks have simply devised spinoffs using old programming they already own (like Fox's Boyz and Girlz channels), or rearranged programs from their libraries on different time schedules.

"I'm afraid some people may be establishing digital tiers as the re-run channels, and those are not worth paying extra for," said Ms. Kresch of PricewaterhouseCoopers.

She also warns broadcasters and cable networks to be aware of what new media providers may offer customers. Telephone and computer companies are busily working with manufacturers to transform the television set (whether it receives its signal via cable or satellite) into the central appliance for all sorts of services—not only for watching programs, but for Internet entry, electronic commerce and even access to telephone service.

In Rogers' view, the cable industry will focus on delivering more channels (a business it has already refined) and the broadcast networks will specialize in high-definition transmission of important or glamorous events like the Super Bowl, and in upgrading some of their library (especially news programs) to digital format.

But the broadcast networks know that the ultimate decision-making lies with the stations, most of which they do not own. Only 43 broadcast stations are transmitting digitally now; another 40 to 50 should be able to do so by the end of 1999.

Will the nation's 400-plus stations eventually want high-definition programs provided by their networks, to give viewers state-of-the-art pictures? Or will stations want to use their subchannels for highly localized programming—news, weather, sports, community affairs or even educational fare—with plenty of spots for local commercials?

For now, ABC, which is owned by Disney, is focused on transforming theatrical movies like "101 Dalmations" into high-definition format, and has already broadcast four of them. CBS Corp. is experimenting instead with football, sending out four National Football League games in high-definition format this season.

NBC has announced no plans beyond converting the "Tonight" show with Jay Leno to high-definition digital transmission in the spring. News Corp.'s Fox says its plans are still in formation, but a company executive who insisted on anonymity said the network was likely to encourage its stations to go the local-interest route.

In general, cable networks, as was the case in their earliest years, are the ones brainstorming ever more finely tuned channels, this time to offer as additional packages to digital-ready consumers.

Discovery Networks, owned by Discovery Communications Inc., and MTV Networks, which is part of Viacom Inc., have been the pioneers, which makes sense, since the costs of generating new channels are better amortized by a company already well established and already producing shows for many channels.

In addition to "the suite"—MTV's name for its array of music channels—the children's cable network Nickelodeon, which is also owned by MTV Networks, will start Nickelodeon GAS (Games and Sports) and Noggin (preschool educational fare) next year, as well as Nick Too, a reprise of regular Nickelodeon but with all shows shifted to different time slots.

The Bravo Network, another Cablevision unit, plans an International Film Channel. Its corporate sibling American Movie Classics has started American Pop, a channel devoted to the history of popular culture. And Lifetime, jointly owned by Hearst and ABC, is developing a 24-hour Lifetime Movie Network.

"What we've created from Discovery's channels is basically a digital magazine rack full of specialty magazines," said Charley Humbard, Discovery's vice president and general manager for digital networks and advanced television. "The person who is an enthusiast of a particular subject will have continual access to that subject, virtually on demand."

But will enough enthusiasts actually buy set-top boxes or subscribe to extra channel packages to make a profit for those who produce the new channels?

Mark Rosenthal, president and chief operating officer of MTV Networks, thinks they will.

"Twenty years ago, when cable started, you had four or five options—ABC, CBS, NBC, PBS and maybe an independent station," he said. "You didn't sit around thinking, 'I wish I had 40 channels.' But when they became available, you re-learned how to use your television. The same thing will happen again."

And as consumers become more accustomed to using the Internet—where instead of hundreds of options, there are literally millions—television providers will start linking their programming to related sites on the World Wide Web, and so will advertisers.

"People sometimes say this is like the transition from black-and-white to color television," said Tom Tyrer, vice president of corporate communications for News Corp.'s Fox Broadcasting unit. "It's not. It's like the transition from radio to television. It's a whole new world."

The New York Times, December 28, 1998
http://www.nytimes.com/library/tech/98/12/biztech/articles/28tube.html

CRITICAL THINKING QUESTIONS

1. Will be the entertainment system 10 years from today be high definition television (HDTV) or standard-definition digital television? Why?
2. Does the evolution toward digital television resemble the switch from black-and-white to color TV or the switch from radio to TV?
3. How could niche-within-a-niche cable channels influence the traditional and future media campaigns of marketers?
4. What are the advantages and disadvantages of increasingly smaller market segmentations?
5. With the potential for more than 1,000 cable-TV channels in the future, how could marketers cut through the noise, clutter and confusion to reach consumers?

STORY-SPECIFIC QUESTIONS

1. Briefly explain digital television's three main uses, as they are forecasted for the near future.
2. What concerns the critics about the expansion of niche-within-a-niche cable channels?

SHORT APPLICATION ASSIGNMENTS

1. In teams or individually, answer the story-specific questions; keep your answers to 25–75 words for each question.
2. In teams of three to five persons, or as a whole class, discuss your responses to the critical thinking questions.
3. Prepare a one-page memo report (200–250 words) to your instructor in which you summarize this article. You will find a model one-page report on the Web site (nytimes.swcollege.com).
4. Write an executive summary (200–250 words). As an administrative assistant to a busy executive, you are expected to summarize selected articles and present important points. You will find a model executive summary on the Web site.

As Band of TV Channels Grows, Niche Programs Will Boom
Lawrie Mifflin

5. Summarize this article (100–125 words) for your company's newsletter. You will find a model newsletter article on the Web site.
6. Individually or in teams, investigate the cable-TV options within your community. Here are some areas to consider in your investigation: Is there more than one cable-TV company? How many cable-TV channels are available? What are the viewer demographics, and associated advertising costs, for the various channels and programs? You may be asked to report your results in a five-minute presentation or in a one-page memo.
7. Individually or in teams, investigate digital-TV options within your community. Here are some areas to consider in your investigation: What is the cost of the various digital-TV models? Are the costs expected to drop? What digital TV set would you buy and why? You may be asked to report your results in a five-minute presentation or in a one-page memo.

BUILDING RESEARCH SKILLS

1. Individually or in teams, create a marketing campaign that uses such niche media as specialty magazines and cable channels. You may create a product or choose an existing product, or your instructor may assign you a product. You may also be asked to submit a three- to five-page policy handbook or post a Web page, along with a letter of transmittal explaining the campaign.
2. Individually or in teams, investigate at least two stores that offer a wide variety of magazines. Your instructor may assign you specific stores. Here are some areas to consider in your investigation: How many different magazines do the stores carry? How would you classify and categorize the magazines? How much do the various magazines cost? Which of these magazines reflect an existing cable program? Predict which magazines could reflect a cable program in the next few years. You may also be asked to submit a three- to five-page paper or post a Web page summarizing your findings.
3. Using at least three other references (e.g., books, research-journal articles, newspaper or magazine stories or credible Web sites), write an 800- to 1,000-word essay addressing at least two of the earlier critical thinking questions. Assume that this essay will be used as an internal reference for a corporation's marketing plan.
4. Using at least three other references (e.g., books, research-journal articles, newspaper or magazine stories or credible Web sites), post an 800- to 1,000-word Web page addressing at least two of the earlier critical thinking questions. Assume that your page will be posted in the marketing section of a corporate intranet.

E-Commerce Sites Target Next Generation of Buyers

By Bob Tedeschi

In their haste to be all things to all people, many e-commerce sites have raced past demographic niches that could hold the keys to profitability. Now as they re-trace their steps, they're finding that one of the most promising groups of potential buyers is comprised of people who are not even old enough to drive.

According to industry executives and analysts, Internet commerce companies are recognizing the natural confluence of e-commerce and the 18-and-under set, and are positioning themselves more aggressively at that intersection.

Given the statistics, it's not surprising. Not only is the current generation of American youths more prosperous than any in history, they are also far more Internet savvy than their elders, having been weaned on Prodigy, CompuServe and America Online.

And when it comes to spending money, they are far from stingy. According to Teenage Research Unlimited, U.S. teen-agers spent $141 billion last year, including $94 billion of their own money—$10 billion more than in 1997. Meanwhile, children under the age of 12 spent $23 billion in 1997, according to the International Data Corp.

Given the fact that so many youth these days are wired, it's a no-brainer that they're spending some of that money online. Peter Zollo, president of Teenage Research Unlimited, said that until six months ago, 4 percent of all teen-agers had bought something on the Web. In the last six months, that number jumped to 10 percent—13 percent among teen-agers with home Internet access.

What are they buying? Zollo said that among teenagers, the online choices are different from their off-line purchases. For instance, off-line, girls spend most of their money on clothes, whereas they buy more clothing accessories online, Zollo said, "because of the sizing issues with clothes." Boys, meanwhile, spend most of their money on entertainment online, such as CDs, videos and games, whereas off-line, they spend most of their money on food.

And although online spending among youths has jumped, industry executives and analysts say the increase has come in spite of—not because of—the efforts of e-commerce sites.

"Web marketers have been more concerned with women than with teens," said Charles Conn, chief executive of Ticketmaster Online-Citysearch. "We're starting to see a lot of interest in parent-driven children's sites, but people haven't done a very good job with teens."

The primary reason, Conn and others said, is that just 9 percent of the nation's 30 million teen-agers have access to a parent's credit card, and as a re-

E-Commerce Sites Target Next Generation of Buyers
Bob Tedeschi

sult, marketers have generally ignored them in favor of those who can easily do business on the Web. Beyond that, Conn said, with the exception of music, e-commerce sites have not been able to effectively market the types of goods that young people are interested in, noting that "clothes haven't worked that well on the Web yet."

Rather than forego customers who can potentially provide 60 years or more of revenue, a growing number of sites have begun devising ways to mine this market. Michael Crotty, vice president for marketing at CDNow, said the music seller is increasingly paying attention to its younger audience. "We're not selling tons of product to them today," he said. "But we need to own the music category for this market, so as they grow and go to college, we'll be part of their vocabulary when they start to buy music online."

To reach younger consumers, CDNow has launched a marketing effort to pitch the company brand to them online and off. For instance, CDNow markets heavily on MTV, with several five-second spots each day on that channel, as well as up to eight 30-second ads daily.

In addition, CDNow and other e-commerce sites are increasingly marketing their products through content sites that cater to teenagers and pre-teens. For instance, under CDNow's partnership agreement with MTV, when MTV.com visitors click on the "music lounge" link, they are sent to an MTV page on the CDNow site that is designed to attract the youth market. "If we dropped them on the CDNow home page we'd lose them right there," Crotty said, noting that the site's home page is aimed at an older crowd.

Indeed, site design plays a crucial role in attracting and keeping younger viewers. Ticketmaster Online-Citysearch, Sega and Nike all plan to redesign their sites in the coming months to appeal to the under-18 set. "Teens see the Web as the arbiter of technology cool," said Bob Lambie, creative director of Nike.com. "We need to be looking for opportunities to be part of that."

For Conn, of Ticketmaster Online-Citysearch, the redesign will yield a "cleaner, faster-loading, hipper site," and will coincide with a marketing effort intended to "make our events better known among teens," he said. Radio ads on teen-oriented stations will comprise the bulk of that effort, Conn noted, "because for some reason we've seen a really good connection between radio use and Web trial."

In pursuing the youth crowd more aggressively, e-commerce sites are trying to strike a balance between making an effective pitch and being perceived as coercing children into spending money. "A lot of society says kids should be outside playing hide and seek, they shouldn't be sitting at a computer making purchases," said Juliana Nelson, senior analyst with the International Data Corp. "The truth of the matter is, they're already making consumer decisions today, so the question is, do you bring technology to them and facilitate that, or not?"

The answer is emphatically yes, said Peter Moore, senior vice president of marketing for Sega of America. "This is a difficult consumer to get to," Moore said. "They're very cautious of hype, they don't want to be told what's cool and they're the most online-savvy generation there is. The computer has been part of their lives since grade school, so it's an obvious conduit to send a message through. You have to market there."

E-commerce providers may also get some help from third-party services, in the form of transaction options beyond the credit card. Seeing the potential for teen and pre-teen spending on the Web, a handful of companies are developing services that will allow young people to make purchases online without a credit card. I Can Buy, for example, allows adults to set up a virtual debit card account at a site, so children can buy independently, within a designated limit. Gift registries on sites such as eToys also give children the chance to choose items, while adults carry the buying burden.

As Crotty, of CDNow, put it, "This is a huge market. [We] just happen to not have all the wires hooked up in such a way that they can transact on a wide scale yet."

Given the number youths already transacting on the Web, however, it seems that younger generations are not waiting for the wires to get fully hooked up before diving into e-commerce. So it's the adults who are playing catch-up to the kids—and in the Internet realm, anything else would be unnatural.

CyberTimes, The New York Times on the Web, March 29, 1999
http://www.nytimes.com/library/tech/99/03/cyber/commerce/29commerce.html

CRITICAL THINKING QUESTIONS

1. How do young people differ in their online versus offline purchasing habits? Would you expect this to change in the next few years?
2. What offline methods could e-commerce merchants use to attract young people to their Web sites?
3. What online methods could e-commerce merchants use to attract young people to and then keep them at their Web sites?
4. Given limited resources, should e-commerce merchants market primarily to young people or to the parents, who ultimately control family spending? Why?
5. What product areas would you forecast as having the greatest e-commerce potential for young people in the next few years? Why?

STORY-SPECIFIC QUESTIONS

1. Briefly explain three characteristics of today's youth that appeal to e-commerce merchants.
2. How does gender influence young people's online purchasing?

E-Commerce Sites Target Next Generation of Buyers 69
Bob Tedeschi

SHORT APPLICATION ASSIGNMENTS

1. In teams or individually, answer the story-specific questions; keep your answers to 25–75 words for each question.
2. In teams of three to five persons, or as a whole class, discuss your responses to the critical thinking questions.
3. Prepare a one-page memo report (200–250 words) to your instructor in which you summarize this article. You will find a model one-page report on the Web site (nytimes.swcollege.com).
4. Write an executive summary (200–250 words). As an administrative assistant to a busy executive, you are expected to summarize selected articles and present important points. You will find a model executive summary on the Web site.
5. Summarize this article (100–125 words) for your company's newsletter. You will find a model newsletter article on the Web site.
6. In teams or individually, review a Web site designed specifically for children. Here is one thing to consider in your review: How does the Web site's design cater to children? Your instructor may assign you a specific Web site. You may also be asked to share your results in a five-minute presentation or one-page memo.

BUILDING RESEARCH SKILLS

1. Individually or in teams, review three Web sites designed for young people. You may choose from the sites mentioned in the story, or your instructor may assign you Web sites. How are the sites similar? How do they differ? You may also be asked to submit a three- to five-page policy handbook or post a Web page, along with a letter of transmittal explaining the project.
2. Individually or in teams, prepare a mock-up Web site that is designed for youth. Your instructor may assign you a specific company or product for which to design the site. You may also be asked to submit a three- to five-page paper or post a Web page summarizing your findings, along with a letter of transmittal explaining the project.
3. Using at least three other references (e.g., books, research-journal articles, newspaper or magazine stories or credible Web sites), write an 800- to 1,000-word essay addressing at least two of the critical thinking questions offered earlier. Assume that your essay will be used as an internal reference for a corporation's marketing plan.
4. Using at least three other references (e.g., books, research-journal articles, newspaper or magazine stories or credible Web sites), post an 800- to 1,000-word Web page addressing at least two of the earlier critical thinking questions. Assume that this page will be posted in the policy section of a corporate intranet.

CHAPTER 7

The Marketing Mix

PREVIEW

The marketing mix embraces the key variables that the marketer can and must manipulate to successfully compete in the marketplace. A *product* must be produced with the right combination of attributes, *promoted* with the clearest message that it can deliver on those attributes, distributed in the right *place* and sold at the right *price*.

Product

Every product has a life cycle—introduction, growth, maturity and decline. Because of every product's inevitable maturation and decline, new product development and planning is essential to a firm's survival in the marketplace. Accordingly, marketers have applied the latest technologies to gauge the potential success of new products, as reported by Barnaby J. Feder in "Marketers Use Virtual Shopping To Gauge Product Potential."

Source: Christine M. Thompson/CyberTimes

Price

From a consumer's point of view, price is what someone pays for the perceived benefit to be derived from consuming a product. In addition to monetary costs, price also can be calculated in barter, time or effort, and even emotion. Price is the only element in the marketing mix that generates revenue for the firm, and the objectives for it can be profit- or sales-oriented. Marketers also take into account their competitors' pricing strategies. A miscalculation of product cost and a competitor's pricing can spell disaster. That is what Toshiba faced, as Steve Lohr's "Japanese Electronics Giants Falter In U.S. Home Computer Market," explains.

Place

Middlemen, retailers and wholesalers who transfer goods from producers to consumers, typify *distribution channels*. The Internet has the potential to radically alter these channels. For example, digital products such as software are sold directly from producer to consumer. Predictably, the old guard is putting up a fight. But as Lisa Napoli illustrates in "Direct-Pitch Stalwarts Reluctant to Sell Online," it's when, not if, direct marketing will prove more profitable online.

Promotion

This last "P" of the marketing mix, promotion, is usually the first to adopt new technologies—especially new communication technologies. Always willing to test new media for its advertising potential, marketers continue to experiment with the Internet. Bob Tedeschi's "Is Coupon Clicking the Next Advertising Trend?" reports on how the coupon, one of the oldest promotional techniques, is being adapted to the newest of marketing platforms—the World Wide Web.

Marketers Use Virtual Shopping To Gauge Product Potential

By Barnaby J. Feder

This fall, like students in many other MBA programs around the nation, 80 members of Prof. Raymond Burke's marketing class at Indiana University were asked to create new consumer products and appropriate packaging. In their case, the assignment was cereals.

The unusual twist here, though, was that 15 student ideas—along with two from General Mills—were test marketed recently in computer-simulated shopping trips. The virtual consumers, drawn from shoppers leaving supermarkets in seven cities from Washington to Los Angeles, were put in front of computers running a program that Burke had created to mimic a trip down aisles stocked with laundry detergent, toilet paper and cereal.

At computers installed in offices at the shopping centers, the test shoppers could pull boxes off the image of the shelf to read the ingredients and, if they chose, to "buy" the item by touching a shopping cart symbol.

After merely reading descriptions of the new products, the shoppers said they would be quite interested in buying the students' most innovative ideas, like a coffee-flavored cereal named Cafe Mocha Crisp. But when they saw the new products alongside old standards in the simulated aisle, they "bought" extensions of existing General Mills brands, like Honey Toasted Chex.

Ultimately, technology like Burke's could find its way into the home and help electronic grocery services like Peapod Inc. greatly expand the tiny sliver they currently control of the $400 billion grocery business.

As Burke's students are learning, though, the technology is already having an impact on how General Mills and many other consumer giants, including Johnson & Johnson, do market research.

"It's been very helpful," said Kathryn Metz, director of marketing research for Johnson & Johnson's advanced care products division. The company recently used simulations derived from Burke's research to figure out how to price Uristat, a pain killer used for urinary diseases.

The technology fills many of the same needs as computer-aided design for engineers, who these days tinker with numerous electronic designs for new products before going to the expense of making prototypes. Marketers can use simulations to study the likely consumer impact of initiatives like discount-price promotions or packaging changes.

There are several advantages. Simulations cost less than full-scale tests in actual markets and test methods can also be quickly modified in response to early results.

Marketers Use Virtual Shopping To Gauge Product Potential
Barnaby J. Feder

Simulations can also allow a company to test what might happen if rivals use price cuts or other tactics to fight a new product or other marketing initiative. Surprise responses by competitors are the most frequent killer of new products that consumers initially embraced, according to Professor Burke.

Simulations, of course, do not shed light on every crucial commercial question. They cannot, for instance, match the accuracy of actual test marketing in determining how well a new product might fit into existing distribution systems. Still, marketers who have used them say simulations are often more revealing than focus groups or interviews.

"It's as close to a real shopping experience as you can get—short of doing something in the store," said Keith Carter, director of international market research for Frito-Lay. The salty chips giant has simulated the snack food aisle in Spanish markets to determine that end-aisle displays spur more sales than advertising directly above the shelf.

Frito-Lay, a unit of Pepsico, also adapted the program to simulate a vending machine to see how likely a buyer of salty snacks might be to choose candy bars, cookies, crackers or fruit instead.

Though Burke deals directly with a handful of big companies like General Mills, much of the commercial application of his work is conducted by Simulation Research Inc., a Marietta, Ga., company that has licensed the results of his past research, freeing him to concentrate on research and teaching.

"We've completed 80 assignments in 10 different countries, most of them focusing on price or combinations of price and packaging," said Steven Nidell, president of Simulation Research. The average test costs the client $30,000 to $50,000, he said. Comparable tests conducted with conventional methods might cost as little as $10,000.

Simulation Research's share of the $4 billion market research industry is barely measurable. Until the new technique's projections build a track record showing they are borne out by experience, corporate market researchers will be reluctant to abandon tried and true methods like focus groups, consumer interviews and actual test marketing.

Consider the value provided by Bases Worldwide, a Covington, Ky., research firm that has about 60 percent of the market for new-product sales forecasting. It simply gives test subjects a one-page description of a product's name, price and features before asking them things like how likely they would be to buy it.

That may not have the visual realism of Burke's technology. But Bases also provides clients with complete marketing plans, based on its research, and has a data base of 15,000 products it has tested over the years to help it evaluate the significance of the answers, according to Mitchell Barnes, Bases Worldwide's director of marketing. Its clients include Procter & Gamble, Coca-Cola and the Kraft unit of Philip Morris.

"I think 3D simulation will eventually be the only way to forecast for some products, but they will be things like automobiles where it could be important to give subjects control over how they view them," Barnes said.

Simulation technology will also be competing for market research dollars with another computer-based approach: online testing of those already shopping electronically.

The online grocer Peapod, for example, already allows manufacturers to perform real-time tests of the impact of price promotions by temporarily posting discount offers that pop up on the computer screens of selected customers. For example, a display pops up offering discounts on Helene Curtis' Finesse shampoos when Peapod shoppers click on Pantene or other rival brands.

But there are situations where even proponents of Burke's technology acknowledge its practical limits. "We won't do tests simulating how products perform on the very top or bottom of a grocery shelf because reaching them on the computer screen is too easy, compared to reaching up or bending down in real life," Nidell said.

And Burke himself is anxious not to oversell his simulated shopping technology, which is still too expensive to appeal to many market researchers. He noted that the $20,000 work stations that he works with at Indiana University's campus in Bloomington, Ind., can handle only a single aisle and 200 products, less than 1 percent of the 30,000 items in a large supermarket.

In the long term, the most intriguing question surrounding virtual shopping technology will be whether it makes the leap from professional market researchers into the home.

"People who don't shop electronically describe something like Burke's technology as what they want," said Frederick Schneider, an electronic marketing expert with Anderson Consulting in Chicago.

Once online shopping becomes routine for consumers, Schneider said, they prefer to do away with most graphics and move rapidly through their shopping list.

CyberTimes, The New York Times on the Web, December 22, 1997
http://www.nytimes.com/library/cyber/week/122297shopping.html

CRITICAL THINKING QUESTIONS

1. Should marketers trust the results of a simulated purchase on a computer screen? Why, or why not?
2. How could simulation technology affect how companies do market research?
3. How will new and improved technologies affect simulation?
4. Aside from simulation, what other product planning tools could marketers use? How?

Marketers Use Virtual Shopping To Gauge Product Potential

Barnaby J. Feder

STORY-SPECIFIC QUESTIONS

1. What are three advantages of simulations?
2. How has Frito-Lay used simulation for product research?

SHORT APPLICATION ASSIGNMENTS

1. In teams or individually, answer the story-specific questions; keep your answers to 25–75 words for each question.
2. In teams of three to five persons, or as a whole class, discuss your responses to the critical thinking questions.
3. Prepare a one-page memo report (200–250 words) to your instructor in which you summarize this article. You will find a model one-page report on the Web site (nytimes.swcollege.com).
4. Write an executive summary (200–250 words). As an administrative assistant to a busy executive, you are expected to summarize selected articles and present important points. You will find a model executive summary on the Web site.
5. Summarize this article (100–125 words) for your company's newsletter. You will find a model newsletter article on the Web site.
6. In teams of three to five persons, brainstorm and develop a hypothetical new product, or your instructor may assign you a product. How would you test market this product with an unlimited budget? With a tight budget? You may be asked to report your results in a five-minute presentation or in a one-page memo.

BUILDING RESEARCH SKILLS

1. Individually or in teams, create a product testing campaign. You may create a product or choose an existing product, or your instructor may assign you a product. You may also be asked to submit a three- to five-page policy handbook or post a Web page, along with a letter of transmittal explaining the campaign.
2. Individually or in teams, investigate new-product promotion and testing in at least two consumer goods stores. Your instructor may assign you specific stores. Here are some areas to consider in your investigation: Make appointments to interview the stores' managers. Ask them how they promote and test new products. Also, what proportion of the product testing and promotion expense are paid by the stores and/or by the products' manufacturers? You may also be asked to submit a three- to five-page paper or post a Web page summarizing your findings.
3. Using at least three other references (e.g., books, research-journal articles, newspaper or magazine stories or credible Web sites), write an 800- to 1,000-word essay addressing at least two of the earlier critical thinking questions. Assume that your essay will be used as an internal reference for a corporation's marketing plan.
4. Using at least three other references (e.g., books, research-journal articles, newspaper or magazine stories or credible Web sites), post an 800- to 1,000-word Web page addressing at least two of the earlier critical thinking questions. Assume that your page will be posted in the marketing section of a corporate intranet.

Japanese Electronics Giants Falter In U.S. Home Computer Market

By Steve Lohr

Two big Japanese electronics companies, Sony and Toshiba, entered the American market for home computers last year with fanfare and high expectations.

The move into home PCs by the two consumer electronics powerhouses has been closely watched as a test of whether these mass marketers of home-entertainment products could teach the computer industry a lesson in how to make personal computers more accessible and appealing.

If successful with their mainstream marketing and user-friendly engineering, analysts predicted, the electronics companies could point the way to increasing the percentage of American households that own PCs beyond the 35 percent plateau at which the industry appeared to have stalled for several years.

Today the percentage has indeed inched above 40 percent of American homes for the first time, but largely because conventional computer companies have been cutting prices sharply. To date, the consumer electronics giants have found their early efforts in the home PC business to have been a humbling experience.

Last week, Toshiba announced that it was ending its foray into the American market for home desktop computers, discontinuing its Infinia line after the remaining inventory is sold.

Yet the move comes just as Toshiba's top-of-the-line Infinia model has received the industry's most sought-after product award, an "Editor's Choice" prize from *PC Magazine*. In the current issue of the magazine, dated Dec. 16, the Infinia 7260 is termed "a classic home PC, well suited for a variety of family users and uses."

The machine, the magazine adds, "offers all the thoughtful design touches you'd expect of a true home PC," including push-button control of a wealth of integrated functions like a speaker phone, CD player, television and FM stereo.

So why would the company drop out of the business when it seemingly had a winner? Well, the glitzy Infinia 7260 carried a price tag of about $3,400. And while most of the Infinia PCs sold for $1,800 to $2,500, Toshiba clearly failed to recognize the impact of machines priced below $1,000, which other producers began marketing in earnest earlier this year.

Toshiba did not have an offering below $1,000, and was severely squeezed by the price-cutting spillover into the larger market prompted by the cheaper machines.

From January through September of this year, machines priced under $1,000 grew from 7 percent of the home PC market to nearly 30 percent, according to

Japanese Electronics Giants Falter In U.S. Home Computer Market
Steve Lohr

Computer Intelligence, a research firm in La Jolla, Calif. During the same period, the under-$1,500 portion of the market grew from 41 percent to 67 percent.

"Toshiba missed the move to lower-priced machines, and the home desktop market is the most unforgiving part of the PC business, where profit margins are the thinnest," said Aaron Goldberg, an analyst for Computer Intelligence.

Toshiba's share of desktop PC sales at retail stores was as high as 8 percent earlier this year, but by the third quarter its share had slipped to 2.3 percent, according to PC Data, a research firm in Reston, Va. Toshiba ranked No. 8 among PC companies selling desktops at retail stores.

For its part, Sony ranked No. 10, with a market share of 1.6 percent, PC Data estimated. Like Toshiba's PCs, Sony's desktop models have been praised for their sleek styling and ease-of-use design flourishes. Unlike Toshiba, Sony remains in the home market for desktop PCs.

Michael Stinson, senior director of marketing for Toshiba America Information Systems Inc., noted that the company had learned at least one lesson about the current state of the PC market. "People didn't want a better one, they just wanted a low-cost computer," he said.

That is simply rational consumer behavior in today's PC market, some analysts note. After all, they say, a PC is a costly product that essentially becomes obsolete every three years. If it is to move into the homes of less-affluent Americans, price is the key variable, they say.

The PC market promises to continue to be a tough one for consumer electronics companies, unless the PC itself comes to resemble a consumer appliance.

"It is a very different business than consumer electronics," observed Tim Bajarin, president of Creative Strategies Inc., a consulting firm. "PCs require a lot of service and support, and the products change every six months or so. The PC isn't a television."

Still, Stinson of Toshiba emphasized that the company had not ruled out re-entering the home computer market at some later date. But for now, it will focus its efforts on the small-business and corporate market, where its notebook computers, in particular, are popular.

CyberTimes, The New York Times on the Web, December 1, 1997
http://www.nytimes.com/library/cyber/week/120197toshiba.html

CRITICAL THINKING QUESTIONS

1. What company or companies could dominate the home PC market in the next few years? Why?
2. What company or companies could dominate the portable PC market in the next few years? Why?

Chapter 7
The Marketing Mix

3. Is Apple Computer headed for extinction or is the company on the rise? Why?
4. In terms of market penetration and price, where could the home PC be headed over the next few years? Why?
5. Will PCs resemble consumer electronics in the next few years? Why, or why not?

STORY-SPECIFIC QUESTIONS

1. Why, in spite of its award-winning computers, did Toshiba fail in the U.S. market?
2. Briefly explain three differences between PCs and consumer electronics.

SHORT APPLICATION ASSIGNMENTS

1. In teams or individually, answer the story-specific questions; keep your answers to 25–75 words for each question.
2. In teams of three to five persons, or as a whole class, discuss your responses to the critical thinking questions.
3. Prepare a one-page memo report (200–250 words) to your instructor in which you summarize this article. You will find a model one-page report on the Web site (nytimes.swcollege.com).
4. Write an executive summary (200–250 words). As an administrative assistant to a busy executive, you are expected to summarize selected articles and present important points. You will find a model executive summary on the Web site.
5. Summarize this article (100–125 words) for your company's newsletter. You will find a model newsletter article on the Web site.
6. Individually or in teams, review the advertisements for PCs in your local newspaper, or visit a local store that sells computers. Here are some areas to consider in your review: Do you find yourself paying attention to the brand name? Processing speed? Hard drive capacity? Price? If someone gave you $750 to spend on a PC, what would you buy? Given $1,500 to spend, what would you buy? You may be asked to report your results in a five-minute presentation or in a one-page memo.
7. Individually or in teams, search the Web for computer bargains. Here are some areas to consider in your investigation: What is the price of these online bargains, as compared to buying a similar computer locally? Would you buy a computer online? Why, or why not? You may be asked to report your results in a five-minute presentation or in a one-page memo.

BUILDING RESEARCH SKILLS

1. Individually or in teams, investigate three computer manufacturers' Web sites. You may choose from popular companies such as Apple, Dell, Gateway, IBM, or Packard Bell, or your instructor may assign you Web sites. Here are some areas to consider in your investigation: How are the manufacturers' Web sites similar? How do they differ? Do their sites feature price more prominently than the other features and benefits of their products? You may also be asked to submit a three- to five-page

Japanese Electronics Giants Falter In U.S. Home Computer Market
Steve Lohr

policy handbook or post a Web page, along with a letter of transmittal explaining the project.
2. Individually or in teams, develop a U.S. marketing plan for Toshiba, keeping in mind that a new PC essentially becomes obsolete in three years. You may be asked to submit a three- to five-page paper or post a Web page, along with a letter of transmittal summarizing your plan.
3. Using at least three other references (e.g., books, research-journal articles, newspaper or magazine stories or credible Web sites), write an 800- to 1,000-word essay addressing at least two of the earlier critical thinking questions. Assume that your essay will be used as an internal reference for a corporation's computer purchasing policy.
4. Using at least three other references (e.g., books, research-journal articles, newspaper or magazine stories or credible Web sites), post an 800- to 1,000-word Web page addressing at least two of the earlier critical thinking questions. Assume that your page will be posted in the purchasing section of a corporate intranet.

Direct-Pitch Stalwarts Reluctant to Sell Online

By Lisa Napoli

At a virtual Tupperware party, no coffee is served and there are no demonstrations of the product's notorious "burp" when properly sealed or how the cheese plane doubles as an eggplant peeler. But Regina Baker thinks her modern interpretation of the fabled American sales gathering is an effective substitute.

"Not everybody has time to go to a party," Baker said. Which is why she built a site on the World Wide Web two years ago to sell her plastic products. She said that the site now accounted for 60 percent of her revenue and 80 percent of her customer base, which has grown to include Tupperware buyers in Japan, Singapore, the Netherlands and Germany—markets far beyond the reach of a living-room gathering near her home in Houston.

But by selling over the Internet, Baker is violating the policies of Tupperware Corp. The company, based in Orlando, Fla., forbids its self-employed sales consultants—about one million of them worldwide—from building Web sites to sell its products, and a year ago, it amended the contracts of its new consultants to reflect the prohibition. Since then, warning letters have been sent to site operators, and the number of Tupperware sites has reportedly dropped from 100 to a renegade handful.

"The Internet is an information source, not a sales source," said Lawrie Hall, a spokeswoman for Tupperware. "We see it as a wonderful way to educate people. The Internet doesn't provide the kind of service we see as beneficial to the consumer."

The traditional Tupperware party, Hall says, connects the customer to the product in an essential way: "At a party, you see more, feel it, understand it."

Though electronic commerce is widely promoted as the Holy Grail of the Internet and the next wave of retailing, Tupperware is not alone in swimming against the tide. Other direct-sales businesses, including Amway, Mary Kay, the cosmetics company, and Electrolux, the vacuum cleaner company, have all shunned the notion of selling directly to consumers online, though each company has built a Web presence for educating customers, enhancing brands and recruiting salespeople.

Several others, including Avon Products and Fuller Brush, a unit of CPAC Inc., are offering their products for sale online but say that is a sign they wish to appeal to the wired generation—not that they are dropping the notion of face-to-face selling.

Mary Kay has developed a compromise approach: For a small fee, it helps its sales force by building individual Web pages on its central computer. To

Direct-Pitch Stalwarts Reluctant to Sell Online
Lisa Napoli

date, 10,000 sales associates in the United States have signed up for the program. But sales are not allowed.

"We wanted to maintain a consistent branding of Mary Kay on the Internet, but this allows them to publicize their independent businesses," said Karen Dodge, a spokeswoman for the company, based in Dallas.

Of the main national direct sellers, only Encyclopaedia Britannica has completely abandoned the notion of direct sales, shifting 18 months ago to phone and online sales bolstered by advertising.

Even in a harried, increasingly digital age, face-to-face selling outside a retail environment with product demonstrations has experienced slow but steady growth. According to the Direct Selling Association, an industry group in Washington, sales of products sold in this manner, ranging from baskets to vitamins to small appliances, added up to $20.84 billion in 1996, up 6 percent since 1992.

Those numbers reflect the need for customer education and personal service in selling some products, association officials said.

"The classic example is Tupperware," said Liz Doherty, an association spokeswoman. "It was originally sold in stores. But people looked at it and said, 'Plastic is smelly, and the lids don't seem to close.' Demonstrations were needed to show the value of the product."

And as for vacuum cleaners, Doherty said, "Before they came out, people used to beat their carpets with a stick. People were skeptical, until a salesman showed up at their door and demonstrated how they worked."

Yet proponents of electronic commerce insist that the Internet, especially the media-rich World Wide Web, is well suited for demonstration and targeted marketing—the next generation of old-fashioned door-to-door sales. They suggest that direct sellers may in fact be holding on to their old way of doing business for a different reason. For one thing, the Internet could wreak havoc with companies that are built on a pyramid of salespeople.

"In many cases, the goods and services facilitate what multilevel marketing companies are really selling, which is distributorships," said Don Peppers, co-author of *Enterprise 1 to 1: Tools for Competing in the Interactive Age*.

"If you're in the business of selling distributorships, you don't want your end users to go around the channels to obtain that stuff," he said. "Amway recognized that right away. What they say is, 'We're selling dreams.' They're selling the chance that anyone can make a business for themselves."

That dream, Doherty said, is the reason that the number of people engaged in direct sales has grown to 8.5 million from 3 million the last four years. That number can be very misleading, however. "Most people who sell it don't last 60 days," said Ken Voght, a Tupperware salesman who runs the Modern Shopping Web site. "They have two parties."

Even so, Doherty said: "It appeals to people for the '90's catchwords: Own your own business, work from home, set your own hours and compen-

ENCYCLOPAEDIA BRITANNICA
Founded: 1768
How it started: Was initially sold section by section. Began door-to-door sales in the 1930's.
Today: Eliminated direct sales force in May 1996 in favor of direct mail, toll-free numbers and on-line sales.
On-line policy: On-line marketing is a major business focus. Also offers an on-line edition by subscription.

AVON
Founded: 1886
How it started: Fragrance given out by a book seller as a gift to women.
Today: Sales force of 2.6 million.
On-line policy: Launched a Web site in 1996, sells on line, allows sales representatives to have Web pages but discourages on-line sales.

FULLER BRUSH
Founded: 1906
How it started: Door to door.
Today: Sales force of 10,000.
On-line policy: Sells on line. Allows representatives to sell on line.

ELECTROLUX
Founded: 1924
How it started: Door to door.
Today: Direct sales force of 15,000 and 500 retail stores.
On-line policy: Bans Web sites by sales people.

TUPPERWARE
Founded: 1946
How it started: Retail, then party plan.
Today: Sales force of 1 million; 7,000 distributors.
On-line policy: Bans Web sites by sales people.

AMWAY
Founded: 1959
How it started: Person to person.
Today: Sales force of 3 million.
On-line policy: An intranet gives distributors worldwide sales figures. Personal pages are allowed but not for customer contact or sales.

> **MARY KAY**
> **Founded:** 1963
> **How it started:** Small retail store in Dallas, individual consultation
> **Today:** 475,000 sales consultants worldwide.
> **On-line policy:** Helps interested salespeople build Web pages for a fee but forbids on-line sales.

sation. With downsizing and corporate impersonality, it is appealing to people."

Tupperware and other direct sellers say they see the Web as an excellent way to recruit new salespeople but most feel strongly that using it to sell their goods would undermine the shoe-leather efforts of their human sales force.

"It would be destructive of morale if they saw us competing for sales with them," said Steven Cooper, a spokesman for Electrolux, based in Atlanta. "Besides, if someone goes on the Web in New York City and sells a vacuum cleaner to someone in San Francisco, and they want to get it serviced, it's not good for customer service to do that."

But Peppers counters that improved customer service is exactly what the Web offers.

"The power of the old way of doing business is not just that I can look you in the eye," he said. "What's personal is that I remember what you like from the last time."

Paradoxically, he suggested, impersonal technology, especially large data bases that link products and consumer behavior, allows more efficient management of customer preferences.

"It's inefficient for the neighborhood bookseller to remember his best 100 customers' preferences," Peppers said. "On the other hand, Amazon.com does just that with every customer. Is Amazon an insidious encroachment on the way we do business? No, they're a rejuvenation, a technologically enhanced form of doing business. It's back to the future, in a sense."

The Tupperwares and Amways could borrow from the Amazon model to better focus on their customers' needs, Peppers said.

To be sure, the Direct Selling Association and its 140 members recognize the Web as a force that must be addressed and have formed an Internet council, which will meet this week to address issues raised by electronic commerce.

While standards are created and refined, a handful of renegade Tupperware salespeople like Ms. Baker continue their efforts, committed to the notion of extending their sales—and in turn, the company's revenue. They maintain that on the Internet, they reach an entirely different audience, one that is seeking products the way they might in the Yellow Pages.

Indeed, most direct-sales businesses have traditionally done little formal advertising beyond listing distributorships in local white pages and have forbidden their salespeople from doing so. The vagaries of the Internet as a medium—more public than a phone number, more private than a billboard—are inspiring companies and salespeople to rethink the way they reach customers.

And while great unknowns loom, there is one certainty, Peppers said: The Internet is only going to become more pervasive.

"Every time someone predicts the technology isn't there yet," he said, "I think about the turn of the century, when people said that the horseless carriage wasn't going to catch on because you've got to learn how to drive and you've got to be a mechanic."

Baker asserted that she was not generally one for breaking rules, and she said she understood Tupperware's position. Yet, she wants to be able to run her business the way she sees fit.

"I just feel we should be able to sell the way we want to," she said. "People are busier now. This is the way things are going to go."

CyberTimes, The New York Times on the Web, February 23, 1998
http://www.nytimes.com/library/tech/98/02/biztech/articles/022398sales.html

CRITICAL THINKING QUESTIONS

1. Why do direct-sales companies object to Web-based sales?
2. How are direct-sales companies using the Web? How could this change in the next few years?
3. Is direct sales a dying or growing industry? Why?
4. How would you suggest that direct-sales companies use the Web? Why?

STORY-SPECIFIC QUESTIONS

1. How has Encyclopaedia Britannica's direct-sales force evolved over the years?
2. Briefly explain the Web-based sales policies of three direct-sales companies.

SHORT APPLICATION ASSIGNMENTS

1. In teams or individually, answer the story-specific questions; keep your answers to 25–75 words for each question.
2. In teams of three to five persons, or as a whole class, discuss your responses to the critical thinking questions.

3. Prepare a one-page memo report (200–250 words) to your instructor in which you summarize this article. You will find a model one-page report on the Web site (nytimes.swcollege.com).
4. Write an executive summary (200–250 words). As an administrative assistant to a busy executive, you are expected to summarize selected articles and present important points. You will find a model executive summary on the Web site.
5. Summarize this article (100–125 words) for your company's newsletter. You will find a model newsletter article on the Web site.
6. Individually or in teams, investigate one of the companies mentioned in the story. Has their Web-sales policy changed? You may be asked to report your results in a five-minute presentation or in a one-page memo.

BUILDING RESEARCH SKILLS

1. Individually or in teams, investigate the Web sites of three direct-sales companies. You may choose from the companies mentioned in the story, or your instructor may assign you companies to investigate. Here are some areas to consider in your investigation: How are the companies' Web sites similar? How do they differ? Do they allow Web-based sales? You may also be asked to submit a three- to five-page policy handbook or post a Web page, along with a letter of transmittal explaining the project.
2. Using at least three other references (e.g., books, research-journal articles, newspaper or magazine stories or credible Web sites), write an 800- to 1,000-word essay addressing at least two of the earlier critical thinking questions. Assume that your essay will be used as an internal reference for a direct-sales company's marketing plan.
3. Using at least three other references (e.g., books, research-journal articles, newspaper or magazine stories or credible Web sites), post an 800- to 1,000-word Web page addressing at least two of the earlier critical thinking questions. Assume that your page will be posted in the marketing section of a direct-sales company's corporate intranet.

Is Coupon Clicking the Next Advertising Trend?

By Bob Tedeschi

Coupon clippers beware: the Sunday paper isn't the only place to find 50-cent discounts anymore.

As retailers wait for the world to embrace online shopping, an increasing number of merchants are turning to Internet coupons to drive customers from cyberspace to more terrestrial shopping venues. Instead of scissors and paper, all consumers need is an Internet connection and a printer.

"In the next year, you're going to see online coupons explode," said Jim Nail, an analyst with Forrester Research. "It's going to be huge."

The primary reason, he said, is that unlike most forms of Internet advertising, coupons provide measurable offline sales results. "Advertisers are saying, 'Yeah, brand recognition is important, but I want to measure whether this ad is making my cash register ring.' This can do it," Nail said. "I can know that Person A saw my coupon ad on Web site A, went to my site, downloaded the coupon, and redeemed it at the store."

Most online coupons are offered through banner ads placed by one of several networks: SuperMarkets Online and Planet U, two services that distribute coupons for packaged goods manufacturers; CoolSavings, which serves major chain stores, and H.O.T! Coupons, which works with independent retailers, like a local pizzeria or an oil-change company.

At SuperMarkets Online, consumers download coupons that can be redeemed at one of the company's retail partners for an overall discount on their next shopping trip. Since SuperMarkets Online is owned by Catalina Marketing Corp.—which offers frequent-shopper programs available in many supermarkets—the online network can track a consumer's buying habits and give manufacturers the means to deliver targeted coupons, either through e-mail or at the cash register.

"It's the perfect one-to-one marketing vehicle," said Will Gardenswartz, vice president of marketing for SuperMarkets Online.

With Planet U, shoppers select coupons for specific retailers, and the company credits their frequent-shopping account at that retailer to reflect the discounted item. For consumers or retailers not enrolled in frequent-shopping networks, the company will mail secure coupons via U.S. mail.

"And future online offers are based on their preferences, so they don't have to wade through the Sunday papers," said Bob Egan, Planet U's vice president of marketing. "Manufacturers love it because we can target their offers."

CoolSavings is by most measures the best known of the online coupon companies. In July, a New Zealand real estate and retail conglomerate bought

Is Coupon Clicking the Next Advertising Trend?
Bob Tedeschi

10 percent of the company for $5 million, just as the site solidified its place within the top 100 most visited Web domains as ranked by NetRatings, a Web audience measurement firm.

One of the reasons the industry is taking off is that online coupons in banner ads generate average click rates as high as 20 percent, while other ad banners rate less than 2 percent—which is also the rate of redemption for off-line coupons.

Another element that makes online coupons so compelling to advertisers is that they serve as a potential avenue for future one-to-one marketing. When a consumer clicks on a banner ad to go download a coupon, marketers frequently offer even greater incentives in exchange for a little information—like an e-mail address or the consumer's shopping preferences.

On the face of it, the transaction represents a win-win situation: consumers receive more coupon offers based on their shopping habits, and coupon companies can sell retailers information about which offers appeal to specific types of consumers. For Web sites that feature coupon ads, such demographic information is the best way to attract advertisers.

As a result, Internet coupons have seen "tremendous growth," said Ann Bertiglia, spokeswoman for the Association of Coupon Professionals. In 1997, she said, online coupon redemption jumped 500 percent from 1996. "And this year will certainly be at least the same growth."

To put that number in perspective, online coupons captured just 0.08 percent of the $3 billion coupon market last year. "We're selling close to 100,000 items a week with our service," said Gardenswartz of SuperMarkets Online. "Compared to the Sunday newspaper, that's a mosquito bite. But add another zero to that, and the newspapers will be sweating heavily."

That next zero may be tough to come by, however, without overcoming a pocket of resistance. While independent merchants and major chain stores like Sears and JCPenney have embraced the concept of online coupons, leading packaged goods manufacturers like Procter & Gamble are more hesitant. Since these companies control much of the supermarket industry, they represent a substantial hurdle for online coupon marketers.

One reason for the resistance is the potential for fraud. Unscrupulous consumers or store managers could easily manipulate an online coupon by copying the image into a graphics program, then increasing the coupon's value. Since packaged goods manufacturers typically repay supermarkets the value of each redeemed coupon plus 8 cents, supermarkets have little incentive to combat such fraud.

The second reason, according to Gretchen Briscoe, a Procter & Gamble spokeswoman, is that coupons "don't build brand loyalty. They encourage brand switching instead."

Another potential barrier to widespread acceptance is consumer concern about privacy. Consumers may not be willing to let online coupon companies track their shopping decisions in exchange for a few cents off a box of cereal.

Chapter 7
The Marketing Mix

Like every other Internet coupon company surveyed, CoolSavings promises to protect the customer's anonymity. "Since our data base is our gold mine, it's in our business interests to guard consumer privacy like it's Fort Knox," said Hillel Levin, the company's president.

Despite these hurdles, Jim Nail, of Forrester Research, believes the online coupon movement could represent a turning point in mass marketing.

"Traditionally, marketing has always been about building awareness, then building preference, then getting them to purchase, then turning them into loyal customers," he said. And marketers have always had discrete programs for those objectives, which consumers eventually stumble onto.

"The Internet will allow companies to zero in and determine where that customer is now, and allow them to respond in real time, to move customers to the next stage," Nail said. "So for marketers, it'll come down to fine-tuning the message to prove to the consumer that it's the right product for them, then fine-tuning the coupon incentive to make it irresistible to buy that product now."

CyberTimes, The New York Times on the Web, September 13, 1998
http://www.nytimes.com/library/tech/98/09/cyber/articles/13advertising.html

CRITICAL THINKING QUESTIONS

1. What are potential barriers to widespread acceptance of online coupons? Why?
2. As a consumer, would you consider online coupons as a novelty, and not worth your time, or the paper and ink to print them out? Why, or why not?
3. As a marketer, would you consider online coupons as a novelty, and not worth the bandwidth and HTML programming time. Why, or why not?
4. Given the rapid rate of technological change, how could online coupons be used for one-to-one marketing throughout the next few years?
5. What are the advantages and disadvantages of online coupons?

STORY-SPECIFIC QUESTIONS

1. Briefly explain the primary reason that online coupons are forecasted to grow.
2. How are most online coupons offered?

SHORT APPLICATION ASSIGNMENTS

1. In teams or individually, answer the story-specific questions; keep your answers to 25–75 words for each question.
2. In teams of three to five persons, or as a whole class, discuss your responses to the critical thinking questions.
3. Prepare a one-page memo report (200–250 words) to your instructor in which you summarize this article. You will find a model one-page report on the Web site (nytimes.swcollege.com).

4. Write an executive summary (200–250 words). As an administrative assistant to a busy executive, you are expected to summarize selected articles and present important points. You will find a model executive summary on the Web site.
5. Summarize this article (100–125 words) for your company's newsletter. You will find a model newsletter article on the Web site.
6. Individually or in teams, visit the Web site of one of the online coupon companies mentioned in the story. Was the site easy to navigate? Did you find coupons for products that appealed to you? Did you print out any coupons? You may be asked to report your results in a five-minute presentation or in a one-page memo.

BUILDING RESEARCH SKILLS

1. Individually or in teams, investigate three online-coupon Web sites. You may choose from the companies mentioned in the story, or your instructor may assign you companies. Here are some areas to consider in your investigation: How are the sites similar? How do they differ? As a consumer, what did you like about the site or the products for which online coupons were offered? What did you not like? Did you print out any coupons? You may also be asked to submit a three- to five-page policy handbook or post a Web page, along with a letter of transmittal explaining the project.
2. Using at least three other references (e.g., books, research-journal articles, newspaper or magazine stories or credible Web sites), write an 800- to 1,000-word essay addressing at least two of the earlier critical thinking questions. Assume that your essay will be used as an internal reference for a corporation's marketing plan.
3. Using at least three other references (e.g., books, research-journal articles, newspaper or magazine stories or credible Web sites), post an 800- to 1,000-word Web page addressing at least two of the earlier critical thinking questions. Assume that your page will be posted in the marketing section of a corporate intranet.

CHAPTER 8

Specializations

PREVIEW

Services

By definition, services are intangible activities that provide customers with a memorable experience. Services are *perishable* because they can't really be stored or coordinated with supply and demand. They are *variable* due to the human factors in production and delivery. And they are *inseparable* because services are created, distributed and consumed simultaneously, and thus cannot be separated from their creators or sellers.

In light of the precarious nature of services, marketing managers must understand customer expectations and train staff to identify and record customers' reactions to the service. The disparity between customer expectations and services rendered often leads to a business's downfall—a lesson that America Online and others should heed, as Steve Lohr reports in "Consumers Are Critical of Online Services, Survey Finds."

Source: Christine M. Thompson/CyberTimes

International Marketing

At the local level, it is a daunting task to monitor economic, social and technological changes, and to constantly formulate the appropriate marketing strategy. Multiply this task by hundreds of additional markets (most of which you have no direct experience with), and you begin to grasp the difficulty and complexities of international marketing.

In addition to environmental monitoring, the successful international marketing manager must heed each country's cultural norms, political subtleties and economic vagaries. The chairman and chief executive officer of Coca-Cola, M. Douglas Ivester, faces all of these, as Constance L. Hays explains in "Global Crisis for Coca-Cola, or a Pause That Refreshes?"

Permission Marketing

Many pundits predict that online advertisements will follow the World Wide Web's growing maturity as a business medium—they will cease to be intrusive and intermittent interruptions of an ongoing media experience and instead function more like invited conversations. In this "new" Web world, consumers would actively seek and ask for advertising materials in a model of invitational advertising originally defined by Don Peppers and Martha Rogers.

It is now thought that to succeed, Internet advertisers should drop their frenetic shouting and adopt a polite-invitation model designed to initiate dialogues with individual customers and keep two-way talk going. Permission marketing, potentially the first goal of every net-savvy marketer, is exemplified in Jason Chervokas and Tom Watson's "In a Web-Centric Industry, Yoyodyne Plies E-Mail."

Political Marketing

The Internet surely has had a significant impact on the way that millions of online users consume information and shop for goods and services. Because of that, its use for marketing political candidates really comes as no surprise. Yet how successful has the Internet been for soliciting votes and "shopping" for candidates? So far it appears that the impact of the Internet, much like that of television, depends on the candidate and the voter. For example, whether the candidate belongs to a major or minor political party has some influence on an online campaign's success. Various attributes of the voter also matter; among them, online information seeker versus a computer-shy couch potato, or a party loyalist versus an independent. Rebecca Fairley Rainey explores the growing political use of the Internet in her article, "From Experts to Novices, Candidates Try Campaigning Online."

Consumers Are Critical of Online Services, Survey Finds

By Steve Lohr

The consumer marketers of cyberspace, led by America Online, have done an excellent job of attracting new customers, but they have an image problem, according to a new survey.

The survey results, to be released on Monday by Odyssey, a market research firm based in San Francisco, found that many of the nation's computer-equipped households continue to view commercial online services as often afflicted with network traffic jams, and slow and hard to use. In the six months from January to July, the percentage of people whose perception of an online service was excellent or very good had declined for all the big brand-name services—America Online; the Microsoft Network; CompuServe, a separate company mostly owned by H & R Block; and Prodigy, an IBM unit.

America Online and Microsoft Network, or MSN, did best in the Odyssey survey—both of them rated excellent or very good by 18 percent of those questioned who had computers at home and were at least aware of the services.

Nick Donatiello, president of Odyssey, said one message of the survey was that the cyberspace services had not really established powerful consumer brands. He noted that well-known brands of mainstream consumer products, like coffee or toothpaste, typically get high approval ratings from 50 or 60 percent of households in surveys similar to the one conducted by Odyssey.

"If toothpaste had the same lowly ratings as the online services, no one would be brushing their teeth," said Donatiello, whose firm specializes in consumer research on technology and new media.

But other results of the Odyssey survey apparently suggest that image problems may not be too important. After all, people are subscribing to online services in increasing numbers—with America Online and MSN attracting most of the new customers—while others surf the World Wide Web using smaller Internet service companies. Once wired, people are spending an increasing amount of time on line.

The Odyssey surveys, based on interviews with 2,500 people, have been conducted at six-month intervals going back to 1994. In the last two years, the percentage of American households on line has more than doubled to 19 percent, up from 9 percent in July 1995. Perhaps more striking, the number of hours spent on line by these wired households has nearly doubled in the last year to an average of 12.8 hours a week, up from 6.5 hours in July 1996.

There are a number of possible explanations, computer-industry analysts say, for the anomaly of online services having image problems yet rising demand, especially at America Online, which now says it has 9 million subscribers.

Consumers Are Critical of Online Services, Survey Finds
Steve Lohr

It could be that the growing numbers of less technologically sophisticated, new online users are initially frustrated by grappling with the complexity of computers and modems. The access providers have become easier to use, but computers are still far more complex than, say, television sets or telephones—the main technologies for entertainment and communication.

"Interactive services are marketed as the pastime of tomorrow, but that easy-to-use tomorrow hasn't arrived yet," said Greg Wester, an analyst for the Yankee Group, a research firm in Boston.

Another possible explanation for the apparent contradiction is that there is a huge demand for new media—a hybrid of computer-mediated communications and entertainment—and people are willing to put up with some technological complexity, even if they find that aspect of the online experience irritating.

Still another explanation could be that the image issue is merely a lingering after-effect of America Online's highly publicized service problems early this year. In late January, after its decision to switch to all-you-can-eat pricing, America Online experienced a great surge in demand, prompting an angry outcry from subscribers who could not get connected to the dial-up service and threats of lawsuits by officials of several states. Since then, America Online has sharply increased its network capacity and, the company says, that problem is solved.

Indeed, the Odyssey survey focused on the image of online services within the industry's potential market—the nearly 40 percent of American households with personal computers. Of those households, 48 percent are on line. The most recent survey, and the firm's previous ones, ask people not only about the online service they may use, but also their image of the other services they are aware of but do not use.

Significantly, the firm's research was not set up as a narrower customer-satisfaction survey, asking subscribers to each company only what they thought of the online service they used. "It's basically irrelevant," said Marshall Cohen, a market research consultant for America Online. "Our data goes completely the other way. Our surveys of AOL subscribers shows that their level of satisfaction with the service has doubled since January."

Donatiello of Odyssey replies that the image problem for America Online—and for the other online services—is a real one. "In the end, behavior follows image," he said. "And our research suggests that America Online's position is dominant but vulnerable."

The gap between rising use and some disillusion with the new online media is part of a familiar pattern, said Erik Barnouw, a professor emeritus at Columbia University and a media historian. With the telegraph, radio and television, he said, it was much the same during the early years of each new technology. "There were absolutely extravagant expectations at first, and you could see the possibilities," he said.

The early enthusiasm, he added, was typically followed by a sobering reassessment, further technological advances, new rounds of enthusiasm and commercial development. "It's part of the evolution of any new media," he said.

CyberTimes, The New York Times on the Web, September 8, 1997
http://www.nytimes.com/library/cyber/techcol/090897techcol.html

CRITICAL THINKING QUESTIONS

1. Should one expect the same ease of use and reliability from an online service that one now expects from a telephone company? Why, or why not?
2. As their brand awareness increases, could cyberspace services have higher customer satisfaction ratings? Why, or why not?
3. What is the relationship between image, price, reliability, customer service and bandwidth (connection speed) when it comes to choosing an online service? Do the factors to be considered depend upon the consumer?
4. Is the gap between reality and expectation for the Internet any different than that for other communication media, such as the telegraph, radio, telephone or TV? Why, or why not?

STORY-SPECIFIC QUESTIONS

1. Briefly explain three reasons why online services are seeing demand rise while at the same time they are experiencing image problems.
2. Briefly explain two results of the survey in this story.

SHORT APPLICATION ASSIGNMENTS

1. In teams or individually, answer the story-specific questions; keep your answers to 25–75 words for each question.
2. In teams of three to five persons, or as a whole class, discuss your responses to the critical thinking questions.
3. Prepare a one-page memo report (200–250 words) to your instructor in which you summarize this article. You will find a model one-page report on the Web site (nytimes.swcollege.com).
4. Write an executive summary (200–250 words). As an administrative assistant to a busy executive, you are expected to summarize selected articles and present important points. You will find a model executive summary on the Web site.
5. Summarize this article (100–125 words) for your company's newsletter. You will find a model newsletter article on the Web site.
6. In teams of three to five persons, test the customer service of an Internet service provider. Here are some areas to consider in your test: Ask an Internet service provider a few basic questions, such as price or level of technical support offered, either by telephone or e-mail. Did the provider respond to your e-mail? If you used

the telephone, how long did the provider keep you on hold? You may be asked to report your results in a five-minute presentation or in a one-page memo.

BUILDING RESEARCH SKILLS

1. Individually or in teams, draft a customer service plan for a specific Internet service provider. Your instructor may give you a sample Internet service provider. You may also be asked to submit a three- to five-page customer service plan or post a Web page, along with a letter of transmittal explaining the project.
2. Using at least three other references (e.g., books, research-journal articles, newspaper or magazine stories or credible Web sites), write an 800- to 1,000-word essay addressing at least two of the earlier critical thinking questions. Assume that your essay will be used as an internal reference for a corporation's customer service plan.
3. Using at least three other references (e.g., books, research-journal articles, newspaper or magazine stories or credible Web sites), post an 800- to 1,000-word Web page addressing at least two of the earlier critical thinking questions. Assume that your page will be posted in the policy section of a corporate intranet.

Global Crisis for Coca-Cola, or a Pause That Refreshes?

By Constance L. Hays

ATLANTA—The World of Coca-Cola, which on the cultural scale falls somewhere between legitimate museum and Disney-style extravaganza, is one of M. Douglas Ivester's hangouts. Once a month or so, he likes to pop in, gaze at the exhibits of Coke ephemera and eavesdrop on the tourists crowded around.

The other day he spied a jukebox, punched up a bouncy 1930's tune, the "Coca-Cola March," and lingered for a moment to listen. "Doesn't it just make you want to get a flag and march," he asked, "and then go attack the world?"

For Coca-Cola Co., attacking the world—with or without musical accompaniment—has become a lot harder lately. Just one year into his tenure as chairman and chief executive, Ivester finds himself leading Coke through extraordinarily bleak times.

Sales have shriveled in miserable synchrony with the collapse of the Russian ruble, the continued economic morass in Japan, worries about an impending monetary crisis in Brazil and an assortment of other ills—even bad weather in Germany.

Gloom would have every reason to prevail in the corporate world of Coca-Cola, a company that gathers 75 percent of its profits outside the United States and is the archetype of the U.S. multinational corporations that rode the '90's promise of an ever-expanding global economy directly into investors' hearts.

But if others confronting today's economic woes seem befuddled—think of the International Monetary Fund, this or that central banker, the hobbled gurus of the hedge fund business—Ivester and his fellow Coke executives exhibit an almost surreal confidence. It is perhaps a byproduct of so many years spent selling a high-fructose, caramel-colored beverage that, by most measures, people can live without.

Ask Ivester about the inhospitable global atmosphere, and you might soon wonder why you even brought it up. Crisis? What crisis? By his definition, it's business as usual.

"This is a changed environment for people of a certain age," he said, referring to the generation of business people who have only known the 1990's expansion. "But for the Coca-Cola Company, it's nothing new. We've worked in these environments for years. We go to a country to stay. We don't go to a country for the good times."

After all, said Ivester, who is 51 and joined Coke 19 years ago, Coke is adept at wringing profits out of its most remote operations—patches of jungle or desert, remote islands and other spots he calls "upcountry." With a touch of

Global Crisis for Coca-Cola, or a Pause That Refreshes?

Constance L. Hays

scorn, he added: "Eighty-five percent of the places we do business in are tough, and they've always been tough. A lot of companies rushed in and got some of the cream that was rising to the top."

It's brave talk. But can Coca-Cola weather so many simultaneous flare-ups when it is so dependent on overseas earnings? Is its bet on global growth so big as to be too risky? Does the situation spell extended weakness for company earnings?

Coke itself is making no predictions beyond the fourth quarter of this year, when it has said earnings will be down compared with the comparable period in 1997. And this comes on the heels of a third quarter in which earnings were down 12.2 percent.

Investors are offering a tentative vote of confidence. With the encouragement of analysts who were impressed by Ivester's calm demeanor in delivering his earnings warning at a meeting in late September, they have bid the stock up from a low of $53.6875. It closed Friday at $67.5625, still 24 percent off its mid-July high of $88.9375.

But the market is not always a shrewd judge when it is infatuated with a stock; sometimes, a rally can lead into a bear trap. Given Ivester's talking down of expectations for the rest of the year, investors are paying a price-to-earnings multiple of 46 for the company.

The risks for companies like Coke are "becoming clearer," said Leah Modigliani, an equity strategist for Morgan Stanley Dean Witter, "but they were really there before as well." Coca-Cola and other global consumer marketers like Procter & Gamble and Gillette may be great companies, she said, but sometimes, "great companies shouldn't really be confused with great stocks."

In Coke's favor are its management, deep with people who have broad international business experience, and its deep pockets, which allow it to invest heavily at any time. Working against it are the global uncertainty that continues to preoccupy investors and the question of whether the company will need to spend abnormal amounts to generate the growth that impresses.

"It's been a long time since they've had to manage through this much turmoil on such a broad-based scale," said Doug Lane, a beverage analyst for Merrill Lynch.

Ivester has the added burden of replacing a legend: the genteel, Cuban-born Roberto Goizueta, who died of complications from lung cancer in October 1997. Goizueta was revered by almost everyone who holds even a splinter of Coke stock for his relentless focus on shareholder value. During his 16-year tenure as chief executive, the company's book value mushroomed from $4.3 billion to $147 billion, attracting such august investors as Warren E. Buffett and anointing new millionaires all over Atlanta and the red-clay country beyond.

Still, the leadership transition was all but seamless, largely because Ivester, as company president and Goizueta confidant, had been integrally involved in top-level decisions for a long time. Among other things, he was the architect of the spinoff and consolidation of Coca-Cola's bottlers that did wonders for the parent company's balance sheet, moving off debt and stoking profits.

A man whose posture and stride bring to mind those polar bears featured in so many Coke commercials, Ivester seems to have blossomed in his new role, exuding a certain charm where he was once the numbers man hovering in the background.

But he now stands alone at the top—he has purposely avoided naming a No. 2—and Coke's numbers are certainly off. Sales volume worldwide rose by only 3 percent in the three months ending Sept. 30, compared with 11 percent in the period a year earlier. And he acknowledged being surprised at the speed with which the global situation unraveled. "I don't think you anticipate these sorts of things," he said.

Historically, analysts say, Coke has used its considerable capital to ride out financial traumas—the devaluing of the Mexican peso in 1994, for example—while smaller competitors retreated or even failed.

But now, with so many problems on so many fronts, the company has kicked into higher gear. There are meetings each week about Germany, Coke's third-biggest market, where concerns include currency value and bottling efficiency as well as the weather, and every six weeks about Japan, second only to the United States in generating profits.

In Indonesia, where sales have fallen by double digits as the economy has tumbled into depression, Coke is trying a returnable glass 6-ounce bottle—a low-cost size—in hopes of spurring a rebound. A car sweepstakes in Germany and coupons on 2-liter bottles in Russia are other strategies in a global effort to improve volume.

With so many consumers chastened, though, Coke faces an uphill fight. In Brazil, cheaper second-tier brands known as "Tubainas" are cutting into Coke's market share. "Coke is much better, but too expensive," said Terezinha Barros Neves, a housekeeper from Rio de Janeiro.

One analyst, Laura Meizler of Salomon Smith Barney, points to "actual declines in core Coca-Cola products" in Brazil, adding: "You will see an even bigger decline in the fourth quarter."

In Venezuela, Coke's anchor bottler, Panamco, has lost market share over the last year to Pepsico, which recently started an aggressive discounting program, Ms. Meizler added.

Coke is reeling in costs wherever it can, from postponing training programs to reducing work by outside contractors. Its bottlers in Japan are being pushed into collaboration: instead of producing every Coca-Cola product, each will specialize in a few products and sell them across a wider region. Analysts say the plan has met with considerable resistance.

"When times are good, you don't think about these things," said Douglas N.

Global Crisis for Coca-Cola, or a Pause That Refreshes?
Constance L. Hays

Daft, Coke's group president for Asia and the Middle East. "Boy, have I practiced everything I've ever learned."

Day to day, Ivester counsels Coke executives around the globe, whom he and others describe as depressed. Don't cancel the Christmas party, he told one manager; it would send the wrong message. Don't take problems like the Russian economic situation personally; instead, he advises his deputies, look for opportunity in the rubble.

"Almost immediately, I started saying, 'Let's capitalize on this,'" Ivester said.

His fundamental tactic is to encourage his troops to share a mindset that posits the company working its way through the current mess and, ultimately, coming out ahead. It is a philosophy that seems rooted in his childhood on the fringes of Gainesville, Ga.

He was an only child, and his parents, both factory workers, gave him "as much opportunity as they could," he said. They also gave him their undivided attention, he added, pressuring him to succeed in school.

"My father's point of view was, if they gave A-pluses and you didn't have all A-pluses, you weren't all the way there," said Ivester, who remains close to his parents—and motivated to win.

"Mindset to me is setting a destination," Ivester said. "It's not a matter of if we're going to get there. It's a matter of when. I've been that way my entire life."

He works seven days a week, often long into the night. His travel schedule is exhausting, too. He has visited 19 countries since the beginning of the year, making seven stops during one 11-day trip in September.

Even outings to the supermarket are research missions: Ivester will often stand at the end of the checkout lane to see what beverages people are buying. Overseas, he has been known to peer into trash baskets to see how people are spending their snack money.

"He is not in the ivory tower," says Andrew Conway, a beverage analyst for Morgan Stanley. "He is out in the field." (Sometimes, in fact, he can be seen driving himself to the field in his bright red Porsche.)

All of Ivester's deputies have learned, sometimes the hard way, that voice mail is the boss' favorite form of communication.

"If there's any relevant data on something, I leave him a message on it," said Daft, "four times a day, minimum, when I'm in Atlanta and five or six times a day when I'm traveling."

Daft once thought he could travel without so much contact with Ivester. The first time he didn't check in for several days, Ivester called to say, "I was really worried about you."

Mostly, though, Ivester's current worry is about how to expand the business. At a billion servings of Coke-owned drinks a day, it simply is not big enough for him. He likes to point out that people around the world are consuming 47 billion other drinks that aren't Coke—every day. It's that mindset business again.

Charles Frenette, who became Coke's director of marketing in May, said: "There is a fundamental belief in this company that we have unlimited potential as far as anyone can see or imagine. It's simply our job to figure out how to remove the barriers to that growth."

Jack Stahl, the Coke group president who oversees business in the United States and Canada, added, "I've never heard Doug say 'I'm satisfied.'" Recently, Stahl got a bottler to increase his sales growth projections to 12 percent a year, from 3 percent. He said that when he proudly reported that to Ivester, the response was, "Twelve percent? That's really just a mindset, isn't it?" It was clear that 24 percent would have been better.

Competitors have a special place in the Coke mindset. Inside Coke headquarters, no one refers by name to Pepsi-Cola; instead, it's "P-cola" or "P-company." And when asked about the competition, Coke executives routinely refer to the power of their own brands, not the threat from someone else's.

But there is much evidence that they do care. Last June, at the Atlanta hotel where Coke was conducting a meeting for money managers and analysts, one attendee was amused by the spectacle of the room-service staff scrambling to remove bags of Frito-Lay snacks—made by Pepsico, Pepsi's parent—from the mini-bars.

Coke, like any other major soft-drink company, would rather have its own products in every nook and cranny—to the exclusion of others, when possible. The practice of obtaining exclusive distribution rights, is at the center of a federal lawsuit Pepsico filed earlier this year against Coca-Cola, contending that Coke used its considerable leverage to force food-service distributors to drop Pepsi fountain products. Coke officials say the lawsuit is groundless.

"Doug's mission is to place that stuff in every conceivable market and to convince people that they should drink it," said Tom Pirko, a New York-based consultant who works with Coke and other soft-drink companies. "There's a belief system there that they are doing the right thing."

Global Depression could certainly challenge the mindset. And the economics of Coca-Cola's business could be roiled by a proposed rule change by the Financial Accounting Standards Board that, if enacted, might force the company to reabsorb billions of dollars in debt that is now on the books of major bottlers around the world.

But Coca-Cola's board offers a vote of confidence in the people it has put in charge.

"Coke and other businesses are being affected by the rolling movement of the Asian flu," said Donald McHenry, a former U.S. ambassador to the United Nations and a Coke director since 1981. "All companies are going to have to

Global Crisis for Coca-Cola, or a Pause That Refreshes?
Constance L. Hays

react and adapt their plans, and Coke is no different." Coke, he added, is "in very good hands."

Indeed, a close encounter with Coke's inner circle leaves the impression that the chief executive thinks the outside world simply needs to follow his example.

"I drink water occasionally," Ivester said when asked what else was on his personal beverage list. Then he said softly, almost under his breath, "Why would you drink anything other than a Coke product?"

The New York Times, November 1, 1998
http://www.nytimes.com/library/financial/sunday/110198invest-coke.html

CRITICAL THINKING QUESTIONS

1. Is Coca-Cola the most recognized brand name in the world? What are some other global brands? Why, or why not?
2. Is Coca-Cola too dependent on overseas earnings? Why, or why not?
3. Would you invest in Coca-Cola? Why, or why not?
4. Why has Coca-Cola been so successful internationally?

STORY-SPECIFIC QUESTIONS

1. What are three reasons for the decline in Coca-Cola's international sales?
2. Explain, briefly, three overseas initiatives that Coca-Cola has started in the hope of increasing its sales.

SHORT APPLICATION ASSIGNMENTS

1. In teams or individually, answer the story-specific questions; keep your answers to 25–75 words for each question.
2. In teams of three to five persons, or as a whole class, discuss your responses to the critical thinking questions.
3. Prepare a one-page memo report (200–250 words) to your instructor in which you summarize this article. You will find a model one-page report on the Web site (nytimes.swcollege.com).
4. Write an executive summary (200–250 words). As an administrative assistant to a busy executive, you are expected to summarize selected articles and present important points. You will find a model executive summary on the Web site.
5. Summarize this article (100–125 words) for your company's newsletter. You will find a model newsletter article on the Web site.
6. Individually or in teams, investigate Coca-Cola's Web site. Here are some areas to consider in your investigation: Does the site have an international section? Does the site use more than one language? What aspects of the site would appeal to non-

Americans? What aspects would not appeal to non-Americans? You may be asked to report your results in a five-minute presentation or in a one-page memo.

BUILDING RESEARCH SKILLS

1. Individually or in teams, investigate the Web sites of three international consumer-goods companies. You may choose from popular companies such as Procter & Gamble, Pepsi-Cola, General Motors or Coca-Cola, or your instructor may assign you Web sites. Here are some areas to consider in your investigation: How are the companies' Web sites similar? How do they differ? Do their sites stress that they are international companies? Do their sites use more than one language? Do the sites offer links to the companies' foreign subsidiaries? You may also be asked to submit a three- to five-page policy handbook or post a Web page, along with a letter of transmittal explaining the project.
2. Using at least three other references (e.g., books, research-journal articles, newspaper or magazine stories or credible Web sites), write an 800- to 1,000-word essay addressing at least two of the earlier critical thinking questions. Assume that this essay will be used as an internal reference for a corporation's international marketing plan.
3. Using at least three other references (e.g., books, research-journal articles, newspaper or magazine stories or credible Web sites), post an 800- to 1,000-word Web page addressing at least two of the earlier critical thinking questions. Assume that your page will be posted in the marketing section of a corporate intranet.

In a Web-Centric Industry, Yoyodyne Plies E-Mail

By Jason Chervokas and Tom Watson

When media obsessed New Yorkers first got their hands on the Internet and began flogging it in a desperate attempt to wring money from the ether, the thinking went like this: the World Wide Web is like TV, sites are like shows, and flashy, colorful advertising will pay the freight.

But while folks from SoHo to Madison Avenue chased elusive ad dollars, a lonely visionary, working in an abandoned warehouse by the Hudson River 15 miles north of the city, came to a different conclusion: forget the Web, forget banner ads; the Internet is the greatest direct marketing vehicle since man invented the sweepstakes, and e-mail is the Internet's lone universal language.

The result was a company called Yoyodyne Entertainment. Spun out in 1994 from an 11-year-old parent company, Yoyodyne creates unique, e-mail-based games and sweepstakes.

The company doesn't just spam the world with junk mail. It builds contests for clients who invite users to take part on their Web sites. Once consumers bite, Yoyodyne engages them in e-mail correspondence that helps the company build a database of e-mail addresses of thousands of people interested in a particular product or service. The company doesn't sell the lists; it sells the notion that it can build a personal relationship between the client and the consumer.

"We ask clients, 'What's a relationship worth to you?' " said Seth Godin, the man behind Yoyodyne. "If they say $7 then we say, 'We'll give it to you for $6." Godin, a soft but fast-talking man of quiet intensity, is something of a hustler of all trades. A book packager by profession with an MBA in marketing and an undergraduate degree in computer science, Godin is also the author of books like *E-mail Addresses of the Rich and Famous*.

Yoyodyne has been Godin's biggest success so far. Earlier this year, Softbank and Chase Capital Partners inaugurated their Flatiron Fund investment program by writing Yoyodyne a $4 million check after valuing the company at $20 million.

At the heart of Yoyodyne's success is a massive data-crunching system called the YEG—the Yoyodyne Engine for Games. Godin says that the system can process more than 600,000 pieces of e-mail a week, extracting and processing words, numbers and multiple-choice responses, archiving responses, and kicking out an array of intelligence responses.

"We built it three times," Godin said. "First we built it cheap, then we built it fast and threw both of them away." The final cost of development was around $2 million, he said.

In developing the system, Godin has had to think through arcane issues that had never been addressed, resolving about 400 separate problems created by incompatibilities between the daunting array of mail readers and corporate gateways that underlie the Internet's e-mail system. As a result, the YEG could well be Yoyodyne's most valuable asset.

"Right now, its perceived value is low," Godin admitted. But he routinely gets calls from companies interested in setting up their own elaborate e-mail response systems, he said, adding, "When they find out what it costs to do it right, they rethink the value of the mailing list all together."

With 39 employees, and offices in Irvington, N.Y., and Boston, Yoyodyne has made most of its money simply selling game services to clients like America Online, The Microsoft Network, Prodigy, CompuServe, and AT&T.

But Godin hasn't stopped at selling custom campaigns to corporate clients. His latest scheme involves using Yoyodyne games to drive traffic to Web sites. The "Get Rich Click" program, for example, is a multi-sponsor sweepstakes guaranteed to drive traffic to sites that are willing to pay 50 cents per visitor. In addition, for companies that want a more traditional sponsorship arrangement, Yoyodyne is creating special games hosted on the client's own site or elsewhere that can be paid for by advertisers.

Despite its suburban locale, Yoyodyne is the touchstone company in the new Silicon Alley race to use the Internet as direct marketing vehicle. It's something about which Godin has been an evangelist for two years, but only recently has he been able to break through the Web-first advertising mentality.

"Six months ago I was very lonely," Godin said. "I was the only one at trade shows saying, 'relationships.'"

Today it can still be a tough sell. "Our problem is visionary customers," Godin said. "A lot of places where I used to go, I'd meet with a 25-year-old who didn't have any money. Now I'm meeting with a 45-year-old who has no idea what this medium is about but has money."

But Yoyodyne could be helped by the fact that other companies are beginning to ply the direct marketing waters. SiteSpecific, a New York company launched as a corporate Web design shop, is now touting itself as a direct marketing company after an investment from Harte-Hankes.

Still, Yoyodyne remains out front in the race. But that position could be tenuous if only because on the Internet, relationships are mercurial. It's something Godin knows well.

"We actually had to put a guy in jail," he said. The man was a devoted player of Yoyodyne games, but after a winner's affidavit disappeared en route to his apartment, he began making death threats to company employees. "He was our biggest fan, yet instantly he became our biggest enemy," Godin said.

CyberTimes, The New York Times on the Web, December 12, 1996
http://www.nytimes.com/library/cyber/digimet/1202digimet.html

CRITICAL THINKING QUESTIONS

1. Is e-mail a more powerful marketing tool than the World Wide Web? Why, or why not?
2. Could Yoyodyne's marketing model be called "direct marketing," "relationship marketing" or "permission marketing"? Why?
3. Would Yoyodyne's marketing model appeal to consumers? Why, or why not?
4. Would Yoyodyne's marketing model appeal to companies? Why, or why not?
5. What type of products would benefit from Yoyodyne's marketing model? Why?

STORY-SPECIFIC QUESTIONS

1. Briefly describe the YEG.
2. Who is the founder of Yoyodyne; what has he concluded about the Internet?

SHORT APPLICATION ASSIGNMENTS

1. In teams or individually, answer the story-specific questions; keep your answers to 25–75 words for each question.
2. In teams of three to five persons, or as a whole class, discuss your responses to the critical thinking questions.
3. Prepare a one-page memo report (200–250 words) to your instructor in which you summarize this article. You will find a model one-page report on the Web site (nytimes.swcollege.com).
4. Write an executive summary (200–250 words). As an administrative assistant to a busy executive, you are expected to summarize selected articles and present important points. You will find a model executive summary on the Web site.
5. Summarize this article (100–125 words) for your company's newsletter. You will find a model newsletter article on the Web site.
6. Individually or in teams, investigate Permission Marketing's Web site. Here are some areas to consider in your investigation: Was the site easy to navigate? What did it offer for free? Did you take advantage of the site's free offer? What was the site's privacy policy? You may be asked to report your results in a five-minute presentation or in a one-page memo.

BUILDING RESEARCH SKILLS

1. Individually or in teams, review Bob Tedeschi's story, "A Growing Ad Strategy: 'Click to Win!'" (CyberTimes, the New York Times on the Web, August 21, 1998), and the first four chapters of *Permission Marketing*. Using this information, create a permission marketing campaign. You may create a product or choose an existing product, or your instructor may assign you a product. You may also be asked to submit a three- to five-page policy handbook or post a Web page, along with a letter of transmittal explaining the campaign.

Chapter 8
Specializations

2. Using at least three other references (e.g., books, research-journal articles, newspaper or magazine stories or credible Web sites), write an 800- to 1,000-word essay addressing two of the earlier critical thinking questions. Assume that this essay will be used as an internal reference for a corporation's marketing plan.
3. Using at least three other references (e.g., books, research-journal articles, newspaper or magazine stories or credible Web sites), post an 800- to 1,000-word Web page addressing at least two of the earlier critical thinking questions. Assume that your page will be posted in the marketing section of a corporate intranet.

From Experts to Novices, Candidates Try Campaigning Online

By Rebecca Fairley Raney

When supporters call the field offices of Bill Bradley's Presidential campaign to offer help, organizers immediately ask whether they have access to the Internet. If the answer is "yes," they are instructed to download the "community involvement kit" from Bradley's Web site and follow its tips, which suggest activities like writing letters to the editor, telling friends about Bradley or hosting a "Dollars for Bill House Party."

The campaign could only afford to print 500 of the kits, but 6,000 people downloaded the electronic version from the Web site within a month of its introduction.

This marriage of traditional and high-tech campaigning came together largely because of the role of Lynn Reed, an Internet political strategist, as a senior adviser to the campaign. At the prompting of Reed, who ran President Clinton's campaign Web site in 1996, Bradley's field organizers were trained to use the Internet to mobilize supporters as readily as they use the telephone.

Giving a prominent role to an Internet strategist is unusual among the Presidential campaigns, however. Although campaign spokesmen are quick to spout platitudes about the Internet's democratizing effects, the use of the medium remains, for the most part, an afterthought. And the emerging industry of Internet political consultants, who fuse knowledge of political persuasion and Internet culture, has been largely shunned by campaigns as they prepare for the primaries.

"They aren't even at the point of asking the question, 'How should we handle this?'" said Robert Arena, an Internet political consultant who ran the Web site for Bob Dole's Presidential campaign in 1996. "They don't see the value in it or don't take it seriously. What's frustrating to me is, it's not like we haven't proven this stuff works."

Whether or not Internet campaigning can actually push a candidate to victory remains unknown as the Presidential election approaches. Online experiments during the 1998 elections revealed that e-mail could be the Internet's greatest gift to campaigns, providing a way to mobilize supporters inexpensively and get out the vote.

But while some campaigns are aggressively building lists of online supporters, others are not even exploring the potential of online organizing.

The campaign of Governor George W. Bush of Texas left the handling of its Internet efforts to volunteers until recently, when a system administrator was hired to oversee the Web site. Elizabeth Dole's staff initially contracted an Internet political firm, but decided later to use a Web hosting company to design the site. The staff of John McCain, the Republican Senator from Arizona, hired a Web design firm, one whose clients include "beer.com." It also used an Internet political firm for technical work on a system for collecting contributions online.

The campaigns of Vice President Al Gore and the magazine publisher Steve Forbes, meanwhile, employ specialists in Internet politics. Ben Green, who started out in the field in 1995 by running an online Presidential campaign for Senator John F. Kerry of Massachusetts, works on Gore's Web site full-time. The Forbes campaign contracted Rick Segal, who worked for the Ohio Republican Party before designing corporate Web sites. Both Green and Segal are consulted by strategists for the campaigns every day.

"It will be a component of a winning campaign," said Bill Dal Col, Forbes's campaign manager. "You can't do it with just television. You have to have grass roots."

Still, among Internet consultants working within campaigns, Reed of the Bradley campaign has the most authority. The decision to place such importance on the Internet was part of Bradley's overall strategy in running an underdog campaign.

"I'm not waging a battle at every meeting," Reed said. "This is the kind of campaign where you can have a conversation with the campaign manager at the coffee machine."

The idea that the Internet could be a powerful tool for building grass-roots organizations crystallized last year, when Governor Jesse Ventura of Minnesota credited his campaign's online efforts as a factor in his victory. Ventura's campaign had no office and just one paid staff member. Volunteers used e-mail to keep supporters informed of events. Just before the election, a well-coordinated combination of e-mail and Web site updates brought Ventura's supporters out in force to rallies during a three-day drive through the state—an event in which visibility counted, because the state allows voters to register on Election Day.

Since that election, the claim that Internet campaigning pushed Ventura to victory has generated intense debate within established political circles. But the methods used by the campaign have been widely studied and copied, and Ventura's experience has served as a primer for Internet campaigning since then.

McCain's Presidential campaign sent a staff member to Minnesota earlier this year to learn how Ventura's campaign used the Internet. But the campaign has not hired an Internet strategist, and the online side of the campaign is viewed as simply a matter of posting new press releases as quickly as possible.

"We're trying to keep our staff very small and invest every dollar we have in communicating with voters," said Howard Opinsky, a spokesman for the McCain campaign.

From Experts to Novices, Candidates Try Campaigning Online

Rebecca Fairley Raney

Even though no one is certain what a national campaign can gain from devoting serious resources to its online efforts, the campaigns that neglect the medium can suffer for it.

Earlier this year, a lawyer for the Bush campaign filed a complaint with the Federal Election Commission about a Web site that parodied his official site. The complaint generated tremendous publicity, sending hundreds of thousands of visitors to the parody site. Internet consultants view the filing of the FEC complaint as a reflection of a lack of understanding of the medium among Bush's strategists.

Bush's official site has had slipups of its own. For several weeks, Web surfers who left the "www" off the site's address, a common shortcut, were sent to a page giving information about the site's Microsoft server software instead of its home page. The glitch was fixed soon after a reporter asked about it.

Nonetheless, Andrew Malcolm, a Bush spokesman, described the Internet as "a major element" of the campaign.

"It will be growing," he said. "It's not where we want it to be, but it's better than it was."

Arena, the consultant who handled Bob Dole's online efforts three years ago, said that the Bush campaign is missing out on the opportunity to build a massive electronic list of supporters that could serve the candidate in the general election. Other candidates started building those lists as early as March.

In the Bradley campaign, the list of 23,000 names collected online is handled with reverence.

"If you're asking them by e-mail to come up to New Hampshire and knock on some doors," Reed said, "then you're using your resources wisely. Our political position requires we do this."

CyberTimes, The New York Times on the Web, August 3, 1999
http://www.nytimes.com/library/tech/99/08/cyber/articles/03campaign.html

CRITICAL THINKING QUESTIONS

1. Could the Internet play an important role in political campaigns? Why, or why not?
2. What is more important, the amount of money spent on an Internet campaign or the type of Internet campaign? Why?
3. How could new Internet technologies affect political campaigns conducted through the Internet?
4. Should Internet strategists have a prominent role in political campaigns? Why, or why not?

Chapter 8
Specializations

STORY-SPECIFIC QUESTIONS

1. The story credits which politician with using the Internet to win his election? How did he use the Internet to win?
2. What Internet controversy dogged Gov. George W. Bush of Texas, and how did he handle it?

SHORT APPLICATION ASSIGNMENTS

1. In teams or individually, answer the story-specific questions; keep your answers to 25–75 words for each question.
2. In teams of three to five persons, or as a whole class, discuss your responses to the critical thinking questions.
3. Prepare a one-page memo report (200–250 words) to your instructor in which you summarize this article. You will find a model one-page report on the Web site (nytimes.swcollege.com).
4. Write an executive summary (200–250 words). As an administrative assistant to a busy executive, you are expected to summarize selected articles and present important points. You will find a model executive summary on the Web site.
5. Summarize this article (100–125 words) for your company's newsletter. You will find a model newsletter article on the Web site.
6. In teams of three to five persons, or as a whole class, discuss how a Web site should ideally be designed to market a politician to potential voters (your instructor may assign you a specific politician). You may also be asked to report your results in a five-minute presentation or in a one-page memo.
7. In teams of three to five persons, or as a whole class, discuss how the Internet ideally should be used to market a politician to potential voters (your instructor may assign you a specific politician). You may also be asked to report your results in a five-minute presentation or in a one-page memo.

BUILDING RESEARCH SKILLS

1. Individually or in teams, create an Internet political campaign. You may choose a politician, or your instructor may assign you a specific politician. You may also be asked to submit a three- to five-page campaign strategy handbook or post a Web page, along with a letter of transmittal explaining the campaign.
2. Individually or in teams, prepare a political Web site. Your instructor may assign you a specific politician for which to design the site. You may also be asked to submit a three- to five-page paper or post a Web page summarizing your site's design, content and goals, along with a letter of transmittal explaining the project.
3. Individually or in teams, investigate the Web sites of three politicians. You may choose the politicians whose sites you are to investigate, or your instructor may assign them to you. Here are some areas to consider in your investigation: How are the Web sites similar? How do they differ? What do the sites emphasize most? What information can be downloaded? Do the sites solicit e-mail addresses? You

may also be asked to submit a three- to five-page policy handbook or post a Web page, along with a letter of transmittal explaining the project.
4. Using at least three other references (e.g., books, research-journal articles, newspaper or magazine stories or credible Web sites), write an 800- to 1,000-word essay addressing two of the earlier critical thinking questions. Assume that this essay will be used as an internal reference for a corporation's public relations plan.
5. Using at least three other references (e.g., books, research-journal articles, newspaper or magazine stories or credible Web sites), post an 800- to 1,000-word Web page addressing at least two of the earlier critical thinking questions. Assume that your page will be posted in the public relations section of a corporate intranet.